"John van Bemmel knows what it's really like to try to share one's faith with the young. He offers insight and perspective for the head, and encouragement and inspiration for the heart. This is a book to read, reflect on, pray over, and share with other catechists. Your kids will be glad you did."

James DiGiacomo, S.J.
Author, *Teaching Religion in a Catholic Secondary School* and *Do the Right Thing*

"...a book of stories that reveal commonly experienced successes and failures, reflected through prisms of remembering, sharing with others, and faith. Each story is brief and could be easily and meaningfully reflected on both individually and in groups. The questions following each story are well written and would be excellent discussion starters."

Janaan Manternach, D. Min.
Carl J. Pfeifer, D. Min.
Authors, *Creative Catechist*

"*Take Heart, Catechist* not only encourages, but enlightens catechists. Through the palatable form of the story, John van Bemmel offers us advice and suggestions, stimulates thought, and bolsters our morale. The stories are intended to be a catalyst for DREs and catechists to share ideas and feelings. Such sharing is a powerful support for those in the challenging ministry of catechetics.

"The book can also be read and pondered by individuals. Questions and a prayer at the conclusion of each story focus on the topic and invite further reflection. A subject finder makes the book even more user-friendly. *Take Heart, Catechist* promises to be a welcome help for catechists at all levels of experience."

Sr. M. Kathleen Glavich, S.N.D.
Catechist and Editor
Author, *Leading Students into Scripture*

"We've all been there—in these well written stories by John van Bemmel. He invites us into religious educators' experiences. What ordinarily are dry topics of methodology and catechetical theory come alive in story form as catechists and administrators come to grips with such topics as discipline, motivation, lesson planning, prayer, discouragement, liturgical seasons, and self-evaluation. These stories put flesh on catechists' experiences of frustration and disappointment, providing a balance of joy and satisfaction.

"The author's practical use of Scripture, reflection questions, and prayer make this a book for your tote bag rather than for your bookshelf."

Dr. Greg Dues
Religious Educator
Author, *Seasonal Prayer Services for Teenagers*

"For volunteer catechists, these stories, particularly with follow-up questions and related Gospel readings for prayer and reflection, will provide sorely needed guidance, support, and assistance.... The author's style in telling these stories—taken from real-life experiences—is consistent, clear, thought-provoking, and rooted in sound theology and educational techniques. He invites readers to immerse themselves in the described experiences of other catechists and to ponder how they would respond in similar circumstances."

Beverly M. Brazauskas
Director of Religious Education & Liturgy
Sacred Heart Parish, Notre Dame, Indiana

JOHN VAN BEMMEL

take heart
CATECHIST

Twenty Stories for Guidance & Growth

TWENTY-THIRD PUBLICATIONS
Mystic, Connecticut

To Laurie

animae dimidio meae

Twenty-Third Publications
P.O. Box 180
185 Willow Street
Mystic, CT 06355
(203) 536-2611

© Copyright 1991 John G. van Bemmel. All rights reserved. No part of this publication may be reproduced in any manner without prior written permission of the publisher. Write to Permissions Editor.

ISBN 0-89622-459-7
Library of Congress Catalog Card No. 90-71135

The verse on page 29 is from *Emmanuel* by Patrick Mooney.

Contents

	INTRODUCTION	1
1	KATHRYN VON ALTEN	6

An elderly catechist reflects on her ministry and is surprised to find that many of her memories are bittersweet.

2	LOUISA MERRIWETHER	11

An experienced catechist encourages a new volunteer to set realistic goals and to trust her own good instincts.

3	WILMA LAZENBURY	16

A beginning catechist learns about the nature of discipline from a veteran teacher.

4	JUSTINA BAUMBERG	21

A day of reflection challenges a catechist to find practical ways to "prepare the way of the Lord" in her life and her teaching.

5	GEORGE BARRISTER	26

Two catechists, one discouraged and the other enthusiastic, discuss ways to develop personal rapport with those they teach.

6   **LESLIE CREWS**   31

   A catechist struggles to express in writing the joys, hopes, challenges, and rewards of her teaching ministry.

7   **JOHN PIMENTEL**   36

   Catechists share insights about the need for silence in moments of prayer and reflection, both for themselves and those they teach.

8   **HECTOR ACEVEDO**   41

   A group of catechists debate how best to incorporate the Beatitudes and Ten Commandments into their lessons about morality.

9   **MARYANN BROUDER**   46

   A parish DRE reflects on ways to challenge her catechists to work harder and smarter at their ministry.

10 **ALICE GUTIERREZ**   51

   A solitary winter walk helps a catechist clarify her goals and develop a clearer sense of direction for her upcoming lenten lessons.

11   SANDRA LEFFINGWELL   56

Two catechists collaborate on lenten lessons that invite children to see God's kingdom as a present reality.

12   RICHARD TORTELLI   61

Time with nature inspires a catechist to ponder the meaning of Jesus' transfiguration and the ways in which he too is being transformed.

13   TERESITA MUNOZ   65

An area coordinator encourages a teenager to give the youth program another chance to offer the "living water" promised by Jesus.

14   KEN SKYROS   70

A youth minister preparing a talk for a regional gathering decides to emphasize the importance of love and dedication in those who work with youth.

15   LARRY PRENTISS   75

An eighth-grade catechist reflects on the meaning of ministry and how best to share this concept with those he teaches.

| 16 | GENEVIEVE CHANG | 80 |

Dissatisfied with the results of her teaching, a catechist begins to understand that Jesus taught his disciples with patience and love.

| 17 | LAURIE MCKENNA | 84 |

Discouraged after her first year, a catechist reconsiders when her DRE challenges her to be a bearer of peace and faith.

| 18 | CLAUDIA BERKOWSKI | 89 |

A substitute catechist, given short notice, comes to terms with a lesson on John the Baptist and gains new insights into John's relationship with Jesus.

| 19 | MAL DE WINTER | 93 |

Two First Communion coordinators share a theology of eucharist that goes beyond isolated, individual experiences.

| 20 | JEREMY NOVA | 98 |

Reviewing a successful class, a catechist analyzes the elements of a good lesson and resolves to learn from this experience.

| SUBJECT FINDER | 103 |

Introduction

The Call

Take heart, catechist! God has called you to this sacred work. This basic fact should permeate and influence, at least implicitly, all aspects of your teaching. It is the fundamental motive that drives all you do as a catechist. You are a catechist, by the grace of God. May you not, then, expect God to be with you in a special way in this calling? When you feel discouraged and uninspired, when students don't respond to your efforts, when discipline problems arise, when you're tempted to believe you are not really called to proclaim God's word in this way, even then God is with you. Do you think God is present only when you feel "apostolic" and teaching sessions go well? As a catechist, you are never alone.

One very important way God is with you is through your DRE and co-catechists. Consider this: after training to qualify as a catechist—doctrine and Scripture courses, teaching methods—you are off to a good start in your ministry. But much more is required as the weeks become months, and the months years. This is a continuing process, beyond catechetical updating, that will renew your spirit and regenerate enthusiasm for your work. This happens in great part when you experience community with other catechists, both locally and regionally.

The Bond

You and all catechists have much to share that will bond you more closely to one another and to your ministry. You can share moments of prayer, days of recollection, and liturgical experiences. But beyond that, you can also share your feelings and thoughts about your catechetical ministry: what has worked well, what has not, problems you face, satisfaction you've known, the impulse to resign, humorous incidents, sources for new ideas or materials, conferences attended, and so on.

Take Heart, Catechist has been written to help you and other catechists take heart by sharing ideas and feelings with one another, and by identifying with the catechists in these stories. These stories about real catechists are intended to encourage a spirited exchange among both beginners and veterans on a large variety of common, important concerns.

The Stories

We need guidelines and manuals to put our concepts in order, to categorize data and summarize knowledge, but stories, long neglected, are needed to involve us personally and intimately in catechetics. Rules and theories don't move us, touch our hearts, motivate or involve us the way stories do. Stories operate within us at a much deeper level than concepts do; they touch universal chords of our human experience. We more readily identify with "real people" in stories than we do with the abstractions of handbooks. We recognize ourselves in stories. "This is really my story," we say, "a story about me. That's just how I feel."

We can better understand what good catechists are, how they work and think and feel, when we meet them in stories. This book—each story, in fact—is therefore about you. You will discover here in a real sense that you are not alone in catechizing. The catechists in the stories are with you—by your identification with them. So are your co-catechists who will share their teaching experiences with you as you read and reflect on these stories, and share your reactions to them.

The catechists in these stories teach on different grade levels, in different settings. Their catechetical concerns, many and varied, include the following:

- lesson planning
- discouragement
- attitude toward teaching
- prayer and silence in class
- personalized approaches
- sharing with other catechists
- catechist as vocation
- catechist's development

- spirituality
- student motivation
- adapting lessons
- learning from mistakes
- relationships with students
- realistic self-appraisal
- preparation for Lent and Advent

These stories provide the opportunity to observe other catechists in situations similar to your own and to consider others' thoughts and feelings, other problems, and sometimes even other solutions. In these stories you will discover not only yourself, but the wider world of catechetical ministry as well. You will resonate to the experiences of others in a variety of situations.

An effect of this will be professional growth not only from sharing with other catechists, but from an awareness that others are in similar circumstances, share similar experiences. You will become more aware that as a catechist you are not alone in your problems, quandaries, or discouragement. You will discover reasons for encouragement, joy, determination, dedication, satisfaction, and perseverance in your ministry.

The purpose of this book, then, is to foster the kind of sharing that builds Christian community among catechists. When you gather to share the stories in this book, together with your own stories and faith experiences, you are, according to Carl Pfeifer and Janaan Manternach, "building up the body of Christ, the community of faith that is the church....The honest sharing of individual gifts in the church of Christ is for the benefit of all."

O*THER* F*EATURES*

With each story a related Gospel reading is suggested for those catechists who wish to reflect on, and perhaps discuss, the contents and import of the story in the light of a relevant Scripture passage. This might serve to reinforce the conviction that God calls you to this work of catechizing.

The section "For Reflection and Discussion" offers provocative questions that may be used with other catechists to promote discussion of common issues and concerns. Used in this way, this book may provide the core of an in-service training program. One or two of these stories may be used for discussion on a day of recollection or a similar occasion, and all or most of them can be used over the course of a year.

The prayer following each story may encourage you—or a group of catechists—to conclude your reflection on the story in a spiritual way. This too may serve to emphasize that God is with you in your call to proclaim the good news.

In the stories there are many topics of prime interest to

catechists, such as those cited earlier. These are listed on pages 103-104 in a section called "Subject Finder." You may use this to help you locate the story or stories in which a topic is treated.

Suitably, the title of each story is the name of the catechist since the person of the catechist is the heart of the story—his or her situation, problems, questions, feelings, thoughts. These titles serve to bring out the communal nature of the catechetical ministry, to emphasize the fellowship of these teachers.

Because *Take Heart, Catechist* offers—through storytelling—suggestions and practical guidance, motivation and encouragement, it is my hope that it will promote your professional growth, renew your dedication, and enspirit you to continue in this ministry—by the grace of God.

1

Kathryn von Alten

Mary of Magdala went and announced to the disciples, "I have seen the Lord." —John 20:11–18

KATHRYN VON ALTEN managed the difficult high step onto the inter-city bus. She took the seat behind the driver and drew a long sigh. Since the testimonial dinner the evening before, she had been rushing. She had packed, slept restlessly, and taken care of leaving Noble, her cat, with her apartment neighbor, and arranged for the taxi ride to the bus terminal. She settled back into her seat, her overnight bag beside her, ready for the three-hour ride to her son's house for the weekend.

It was hard for Kathryn not to feel a good deal of satisfaction and pleasure at this moment. Last evening she had been recognized by her parish for her 21 years in religious education, four of them as a secretary and the rest as a catechist. Who would have thought of a long tenure as a catechist when a DRE years ago asked her secretary to fill in for an absent teacher? Yet that is how God had touched Kathryn's life and led her, through years of surprise, satisfaction, disappointment, and joy, to touch the lives of hundreds of children, parents, and associates in ministry.

As the bus lumbered away from the terminal, Kathryn reached for her bag and took out the certificate of appreciation. She read it slowly, almost out loud: "The people of Saints Cosmos and Damian Parish express their deep appreciation to Kathryn Frances von Alten for twenty-one years of devoted service as a catechist." She was deeply moved by this sign of appreciation and even by a parish dinner in her honor, but she had been rather embarrassed by the speeches. "They made too much of my teaching," she thought, but quickly realized that the appreciation may have been as much for the quantity of her catechetical work as for its quality. She knew as well as anyone that catechists, as a rule, don't stay very long. She had seen so many come and go.

Kathryn was looking out the window as the bus squeezed into the interstate traffic, but she wasn't really looking at anything. Her memories were rushing past her as rapids cascade past an eddy. It surprised her that many of them were of struggle, of disappointment, of frustration, of failure, at least as she perceived it. "Pleasant memories," she said to herself wryly. She thought it ironic that although she was feeling generally pleased with the work of all those years, with the good evaluations she had received, with the many favorable comments the night before—with what had to be judged a successful and satisfying "career"—she was immersed in memories of the price she had paid.

Her clearest recollections were of the two times she had almost quit. On one occasion, she was exasperated by the mandate from the pastor to use a new textbook series, one that she and the evaluation committee had judged to be "inappropriate and injurious" to the children. The manner in which this decision had been handed down still disturbed her. On another occasion, Kathryn found herself in a stinging controversy between the parish council's education committee and a group of parents who disapproved of the teaching by three catechists. Kathryn was one of them. "Our children are not being taught the doctrines of the church," the parents had said. The DRE mediated the dispute, but Kathryn felt hurt and was determined that that year would be her last. But it wasn't—hardly.

How often, Kathryn recalled more by impression than by count, she had been discouraged and even upset by the absence in her students of any enthusiasm, not to say interest. And this happened week after week (she knew she exaggerated). She remembered times she prepared her classes thoroughly, only to have them end up flat. She seldom knew why, really; it just happened.

The spring sun was sitting on the horizon now and shone brightly on Kathryn. She looked at her watch. More than an hour's ride yet. She remembered traveling to conventions and workshops, taking courses for her catechist certification, reading more books than she dared to recall. Such demands, it seemed, were only recent. In the early years, very little was asked of her by way of professional growth. "You get what you pay for" went through her mind.

It surprised Kathryn that isolated conversations came back to her, even from the early years: listening to children's excuses for not doing assignments, hearing of family problems and even tragedies, reprimanding students for misbehaving, exhorting them to modest effort, calling parents about their children.

If anyone had a broad view about being a catechist, Kathryn did. She shifted in her seat and thought about this stream of struggles that flowed past her. She recalled difficulties and disappointments, the discouragement, the demands on her time—all, it seemed, a natural part of her ministry.

That was the realization that washed over Kathryn's mind and settled in gently, as waves, broken on the beach, sink into the sand. On the whole, Kathryn was more aware of the joys of the past two decades. She thought of the deep satisfaction she experienced; the gratitude expressed by children, parents, and co-catechists; the rewards of her dedication; the spiritual growth she witnessed in her students and in herself—all memories she would cherish. How many she had recalled the evening before!

These two elements of her career, the struggle and the satisfaction, seemed to fill Kathryn's being. As never before, she saw—felt—the connection between them, how one led to the other, how strife and striving were the cost of true satisfaction. She was aware that it had taken her a long time to grasp and embrace the truth of her Lord's resurrection lesson. She saw all her catechetical efforts in that light, that so much good came when and because she gave herself to the ministry God had called her to 21 years earlier. Feeling good about the honor given her, Kathryn gazed over the farmland as the bus sped through the lowering darkness.

For Reflection and Discussion

1. What are your feelings about being a catechist for at least ten more years? Why do you feel this way?

2. Do you think Kathryn's catechetical "career" is realistically described? Why? Why not?

3. Do you sympathize with Kathryn? Do you recognize your own teaching experience in hers?

4. Do you tend to dwell on the negative and difficult side of teaching, or neglect or underestimate the positive?

5. What resurrection results do you believe will come from the "passion" you experience in your teaching?

PRAYER

I am grateful, God, that you are with me in the trials and joys of being your catechist. By your grace, may I be more willing in the coming years to pay the price of being a dedicated catechist. May I finally learn that you are with me to get *through* trials, not to *escape* them. Amen.

2

Louisa Merriwether

Which of you, intending to build a tower, would not first sit down and work out the cost to see if there was enough to complete it? —Luke 14:25–33

LOUISA MERRIWETHER walked slowly along the hallway of St. Martin's Parish Center, straightening out her notepapers and books. The last class of the catechist preparation program had just ended, and her thoughts were on the year of catechizing that lay ahead. She had taught second graders years ago before she was married, and she felt almost embarrassed by her lack of training then. "What a difference in attitude," she said to herself.

Louisa stood by the door a moment, finding her jacket and nodding to her colleagues as they left. She noticed Beth just leaving the ministry office and waited for her. Beth would be teaching the other sixth grade, as she had for the past five years. Louisa felt good talking with Beth about her teaching experience. She had much to share, and Louisa was always eager to learn what she could from others about teaching. She welcomed occasions when catechists shared their preparation and classroom experiences. "Every parish needs a Beth," Louisa mused.

"Beth, do you have to get right home? How about some coffee at Henry's?"

"Love to," Beth replied. "Sounds great."

At Henry's, they sat at a booth and quickly gave their orders.

"Beth, I've completed the certification course and I'm supposed to be ready for the year, but I'm really nervous. I really don't feel good about all this."

"You are ready," Beth interrupted, "as ready as you can reasonably expect." She paused a moment, then added, "Look, you've done well in this course, you've got some experience, and you're open to learning from your experience and even from your mistakes. More than that, you like kids and get along with them. I can see that in the neighborhood."

"I know it's different with kids in class." The waitress placed the coffee and onion rings on the table. Beth smiled at her and continued. "But all your experiences can help to make you a better catechist, including those with the kids at home and around the neighborhood. Really."

Their conversation drifted off to a quick succession of other topics: the sewer construction, Herb Daly's accident, and the Labor Day parade. Beth found herself staring out the window for a moment and then turned to Louisa.

"You know, I think I've learned something that's helped me a lot in catechetics. I guess it seeped in from these years of teaching. It has to do with what I call the long-range view. It's different from...it's more than long-range planning. It's really an attitude, a frame of mind about teaching religion."

Louisa put her cup down and sat back, listening intently. "Go on, Beth. What is this attitude?"

"I was reminded of it Sunday, listening to the Gospel. It's an attitude of realism, I guess. That Gospel episode—Luke, isn't it? It was the one about being prepared, realizing what some project is going to cost in terms of money and personal energy, knowing very clearly what the objective is, and wanting it enough to put up with all the problems and disappointments you know will come with it. The Gospel had to do with building a tower and knowing all the costs ahead of time." Beth leaned forward. "The one part ended, 'That man began to build what he could not finish.'"

Louisa was not quite sure of Beth's point. She waited for her to continue.

"What I think is so important as you start this work is to be very realistic. You have to be very honest with yourself about what you want to achieve, what it will cost, and you have to decide now if it's worthwhile enough to pay the price.

"This certification course and your teacher's manual are a help toward knowing your goal, but that is something you have to make your own, to make very meaningful to yourself. You have to think about it often and pray over it.

"The goal can be so noble and uplifting, but when discouragement comes, it has to be real enough and desirable enough to keep you pressing on toward it—for God's sake, the kids', and your own. Louisa, you know the kinds of problems that can come up." Beth ticked them off on her fingers: "discipline, blank faces and total disinterest, lack of parental interest even, not enough time to prepare, not enough class time. To be realistic, problems will come up that you haven't even heard of. The point is, you have to be aware now that these hard times will come, but keep your eye—and heart—on the goal you set, and try to anticipate and minimize the problems through your hard work and preparation.

"Louisa, in a way, it's like any other job; the goal, what your heart is set on, has to make it all worthwhile. The trick is to develop this long-range attitude through your class preparation, other reading, discussion, and prayer, so that it's in your blood, a part of you. It will help you not only survive some of the inevitable problems, it will even prevent some of them from ever coming up."

They sat quietly for a moment, Louisa looking off across the floor, biting her lower lip. She turned to Beth. "What you say makes a lot of sense, I know. But you didn't get this idea before you ever set foot in a classroom, did you?"

"My goodness, no, I worked toward this, I guess imperceptibly. The attitude developed slowly, and only after some mistakes and a lot of discouragement. I wanted to quit more than once in my early years. Louisa, you're going to make mistakes and do an awful lot of learning, but I think the sooner you start to link your catechist work with that Gospel, the better. Look, you'll be willing to give time to this work, you'll study, you'll pray and be open to the Spirit. Really, you'll be fine, but don't let your long-range goal get away from you."

Louisa remained silent. She felt enthusiastic, but still nervous. She signaled for the check.

For Reflection and Discussion

1. How would you express how Louisa feels about the upcoming year of teaching?

2. What are your feelings about beginning a new catechetical year?

3. If you were Beth, what would you tell Louisa?

4. If you are not a first-year catechist, how has your attitude about teaching changed from one year to the next?

5. Describe a catechetical occasion when you had to decide if you were willing to push yourself for a worthwhile goal. How did your thinking go?

Prayer

Enlighten me, God, about what I really want to accomplish as your catechist. Awaken me to the price I may have to pay, and strengthen my resolve to labor for your reign and not to count the cost. Amen.

3

WILMA LAZENBURY

"Go, therefore, and make disciples of all nations, baptizing them in the name of the Father, and of the Son, and of the holy Spirit." — Matthew 28:19

WILMA LAZENBURY stopped walking and tapped her husband's arm as a gull circled briefly and lighted on a rock just a few yards from them. She and Paul took the one-mile cliff walk at least once every vacation, walking along the narrow macadam path some thirty feet above where the waves broke boldly against the rocky shore.

The Labor Day afternoon was chilly and overcast, with the smell of seaweed heavy in the air. Wil and Paul would be heading home the next day.

"Fourteenth year," Wilma announced. "I can't believe you're starting your fourteenth year teaching at Custer Junior High."

"Time flies…" Paul said, and then added quickly, "but what about you? In three weeks you'll be starting your first year as a catechist at St. Anastasia. You must be excited about it. Your catechist courses are over, and those fifth graders don't know how lucky they are."

"Well, I feel pretty good about it, but I sometimes wonder about some of the stories I hear about kids' behavior," Wilma admitted. "That part of being a catechist frightens me a little. What if I can't handle them?"

"Not to worry, Wil," Paul said, trying to reassure her. "One thing I've learned from my years of teaching is that those stories are the exceptions, and are probably exaggerated. Besides, good teachers don't have discipline problems, at least not habitually. You'll see."

They came upon a slat bench and sat down, gazing for a while in silence at the expanse of gray ocean and sky before them.

"Did you ever think, Wil, that as a catechist you'll develop disciples of Jesus"—he emphasized *disciples*—"and that discipline is needed?" He stressed *discipline*. "There's a real connection between 'discipline' and 'disciple.'" He turned to face his wife. "You know, a disciple is someone who has absorbed the teachings of another and wants to follow that person. Well, the disciple has to be open to that teaching. There has to be a certain self-control in the would-be disciple, an interior disposition eager to receive the teaching. This self-control, this receptive attitude is discipline."

Wil shook her head and objected, "But don't most people understand discipline as what a teacher does to ensure or even enforce students' conformity to class rules?"

"I know," Paul said, "but that's part of the problem. Try to think of discipline as motivating student interest and receptivity, not as forcing a minimal behavior. Discipline is in the student, not in the teacher. An interesting, challenging, and respectful catechist heads off behavior problems before they begin. That's why you should do just fine, Wil. You've been working hard with lesson planning and background reading."

Wil looked out toward the horizon for a while, then stood up. "Let's move along, Paul," she said.

Paul stood up and took her hand. "I didn't have these ideas about discipline my first day of teaching, you know. The best ideas come through teaching experience; there's lots of trial and error. It takes time and you will make mistakes, but I think that if you have the right attitude about discipline it will help a lot."

"What you've said is helpful, Paul, but I'm still a bit nervous about it. With my courses I'll be pretty well prepared, but...." A gull squawked boisterously as it chased another gull from a clam it had just dropped on the rocks. Wil and Paul turned to observe the squabbling.

As she watched, Wil couldn't remember any real discussion about discipline in her catechetical courses, where only a few incidental remarks were made. Most of the talk about disruptive behavior came in the form of exaggerated tales that the beginning catechists repeated among themselves. She was amused by the thought that although these stories about discipline problems were clearly overblown, they were still "real" enough to frighten her.

"Anyway, Paul," Wil resumed, her mind back on their conversation, "what else can you tell me about discipline? What have you found helpful?"

"There are so many things you pick up as you go along." Paul looked about him. "For instance, don't ever be confrontational like those two gulls. Don't let a student lead you into arguing or being sarcastic. Settle a serious point later on, in private." He thought about his own experience as they walked on.

"Be very clear about what you expect in your class sessions, about your reasons for various rules. When you must call attention to something disruptive, do it gently and respectfully. Oh, and be kind of easy about what misbehavior you want to interrupt your teaching for. You'll learn what infractions are worth bothering about. Sometimes a brief pause and a glance at a student will be enough to handle a minor point."

They reached the highest point along the walk where there was a telescope and two benches. On other days they had sat there for long periods, mostly in silence. From there the path descended gradually to a parking lot.

Paul continued. "One more thing, Wil, that I think will help. Use silence when you start a session. Have some reason—prayer included—for the kids to be still, to sit quietly even for fifteen seconds. Before the silence they can chat and laugh as they assemble, but after the silence they'll know that class has begun and certain things are expected of them. Their interest in what you're saying and doing will take over at that point."

Wil looked skeptical and Paul sensed that his suggestions might seem bewildering to her. He was anxious to end the conversation in an upbeat way. "Wil, I think you'll find that a good catechist is not going to run habitually into 'discipline problems,' but at the same time will be ready for an occasional disruptive incident. There's so much you'll pick up from your experiences and from sharing ideas with other catechists, and sometimes you'll come across helpful books and articles."

He stopped walking, took Wilma's arm, and smiled. "The

main thing, Wil, is to think of discipline in a positive way: as building the right atmosphere for learning, as a way of fostering self-control in students who at least implicitly want to be open to becoming disciples of Jesus...."

As they crossed the parking lot to their car, it began to drizzle. Wilma loved the cool rain on her face, their traditional walk, and today, noticing a hint of clearing in the western sky, she felt particularly good.

*F*OR *R*EFLECTION AND *D*ISCUSSION

1. In what way, if any, has your basic understanding of discipline changed since reading this story?

2. In what way(s) concerning discipline do you identify with Wilma?

3. What apprehensions about discipline did you have before teaching that you now find were unfounded or exaggerated?

4. What advice concerning discipline would you give a beginning catechist?

5. If you have some catechetical experience, what three practical suggestions would you make to a beginning catechist?

*P*RAYER

Grace me, God, with the good sense to treat those I teach with love and deep respect. Help me to become more disciplined in my own life so that I may be a better tool in your hands to guide others to you. Amen.

4

Justina Baumberg

A voice cries out in the desert: prepare the way of the Lord! Make straight in the wasteland a highway for our God. —Matthew 3:1–6

JUSTINA BAUMBERG swept around a curve on Route 16. It was a clear December afternoon and the sun was setting behind the Presidential Range of the White Mountains. Her face broadened into a smile as she thought about the day's theme. She had just come from the parish day of recollection for catechists, and the imposing silhouette of the mountain range and the snow-covered intervening hills now in partial shadow seemed an appropriate part of it. It crossed her mind to stop for a short while to absorb the stark beauty from the roadside, but she was expected home shortly and darkness would fall suddenly on the mountain roads once the sun dropped behind the hills.

"Hills," she said to herself with amusement. "Every valley shall be filled in, and every mountain and hill shall be made low. Prepare the way of the Lord." Justina thought it humorous to imagine the almost unimaginable task of smoothing out those hills in front of her and filling in the gorges and valleys. But she was quick, even if reluctant, to see a connection, as awesome as the hills, between leveling this land and her catechetical work. Both led her to think of preparing "the way of the Lord"; one was described in Scripture, the other was worked out week after week with her class.

This day of recollection theme, taken from the day's liturgy at the parish center, was well suited to catechists: Prepare the way of the Lord. But there was much more to it than that. Its meaning was richer by far than simply a call in the desert from John the Baptist. He was quoting Isaiah and referring to Jesus. But what of the strange imagery in Isaiah that John alludes to? A highway made straight, valleys filled in, mountains made low?

In 587 B.C., Justina recalled, Babylon destroyed Jerusalem, and the Israelites were taken into exile, a shattering disaster politically and religiously. For two generations in exile, they struggled with the question of God's presence ("presence" was almost God's name!). They wrestled with despair; God's judgment was decisive and severe.

But there was a voice of hope in the land, Isaiah's. He announced the good news that God would save the people once more. They would return to their land; their kingdom and temple would be restored. There would be a new deliverance, a new intervention by God in their history.

To describe God's coming, Isaiah's impassioned poetry uses the image of a king's grandiose travel: a road prepared to make the journey as comfortable and dignified as possible—a straight and level route. In Isaiah's imagery, even the hills are to be leveled, the valleys filled in, the way made straight—a super-highway laid across the desert to prepare for the Lord's coming as he led the people to salvation. John used this imagery to speak of Jesus, "the one who is to come."

Justina thought she would always think of Isaiah's imagery when she looked at her native hills. "Some job that would be," she thought as she pictured Isaiah's image taken literally. It was almost dark as she coasted down the long hill toward town.

Justina had found the day of recollection useful and stimulating, even though, as often before, she had to push herself to go. The liturgy, the talks, and the discussions with her associates served to clarify the motivation for their ministry. What are we trying to accomplish in our catechetical work? She thought this a very good topic for a mid-year taking-stock. And the idea of linking that to the Gospel was right on the mark.

She recalled many of the catechetical goals that were mentioned. To develop values consistent with the Gospels. To be a pray-er. To make sense out of life. To recognize the presence of Jesus in life. To esteem our Catholic faith-heritage. To be sensitive to the call of God. To work for a more Christ-like neighborhood and world. To be fundamentally justice- and love-oriented. To mature as a person and as a Christian. To appreciate the liturgy. To search for God in truth. To learn about religious faith as practiced by various people at different times. Justina was surprised at how many she could remember. Scarcely any she had heard could be disregarded, and yet some seemed more important, more to the heart of the matter, than others.

The street lights were on as Justina turned into town. She

had felt moved when she heard, and now as she recalled, the many goals she and her co-catechists were working to achieve. Actually, she was impressed, even awed, at what they were all trying to accomplish, but she knew as well as she knew her own street that she and the others were the tools through whom the Spirit worked to make such goals incarnate.

Looking back, Justina thought it strange that no one had mentioned the day's theme, to prepare the way of the Lord, as one of the goals of catechetics. "Perhaps they all just presumed that that was one of them," she thought. The question stood large in her mind. "Is it the main one?" She wished it had come up expressly at the discussions. She wanted to think more about it, but she was almost home. "When you get right down to it, what else are we trying to do but to teach children to open themselves to God's presence and activity in their lives...to prepare the way of the Lord?"

Justina pulled into the driveway and went in the side door where her husband, Leo, greeted her. "Hi. How did it go?"

"Hills," Justina replied.

For Reflection and Discussion

1. Have you ever seriously thought about what you are trying to accomplish in your catechetical work? How recently have you done this?

2. What are at least five of your goals as a catechist? Write them down.

3. Are there days of recollection for catechists in your parish? If so, do you attend regularly? If there are none, why not suggest that one be scheduled?

4. What difference would it make in your teaching if you viewed your work as "preparing the way of the Lord"? What are some examples?

PRAYER

God, there are so many goals I want to reach in my work as your catechist. Grant me the wisdom, through the abiding presence of your Spirit, to keep in mind, above all, that I am helping prepare the way for your reign. Amen.

5

GEORGE BARRISTER

And coming to her, Gabriel said, "Hail, favored one. The Lord is with you." —Luke 1:26–38

GEORGE BARRISTER sat down in the diner with his fellow high school catechist. He was thinking of telling the waitress he'd like to order "one grateful student, with a side order of satisfaction." He looked up at Roger, who was taking off his down jacket, and felt compelled to tell him he was really thinking about making this, his third year as a catechist, his last. "Uneventful" came to mind to describe not only the class just concluded, but his whole teaching experience. He even considered the word an understatement, pure and simple.

Before he could speak, Roger had slid into his seat and started talking. "Those kids are real nuts, George. You should have seen them tonight. When I walked into class, I thought they'd greet me with comments about the Christmas party we had. Instead, they were all in the usual semicircle, but they were all sitting up straight, feet together, hands folded on desks, staring at a point over my head like robots. I didn't even notice it at first, but when I did I stopped in mid-sentence. They burst out laughing. Really funny! And yet when we got into our discussion on what difference the incarnation makes, they got right into it....How did your class go?"

"Okay, I guess," George said. He enjoyed Roger's story and his enthusiasm, but they only served as an introduction to his feelings about being a catechist. "I'm not coming back next year; I've had enough."

The waitress put down two glasses of water and took their orders. When George gave his, he added, "and a side order of satisfaction." Then he quickly suggested she disregard that part.

Responding to Roger's questioning look, George leaned forward and went on. "It's just that this isn't for me. I can't make it go. I know I prepare well. I bone up on the subject matter, read around it, draw up lesson plans, and use the class time very well. I think I'm intent in each class, but I run into heavy doses of lethargy and a lack of responsiveness." He leaned back and sipped some water. "By and large, this is true class after class. There's something missing, I know. I don't think anybody packs more information into a class," he added.

After a moment's silence—Roger was listening intently—George went on. "I know I'm all business in a class, but that's not the problem, at least not completely. I know for sure that I'm not as easy-going as you are, but what I realized just now, hearing your story, is that students don't even attempt to be funny in my class."

The waitress placed their orders on the table and Roger asked for ketchup. He assured George that the kids appreciated how well prepared he was, that it had to come through to them that their catechist was dedicated to his work, and that his faith was important to him. "That has to count for something, George, a whole lot."

George nodded and waited for Roger to go on. "I wonder, George, if what you've described is related to your relationship to your students. There's nothing wrong with being serious—you don't have to be as informal as I am—but they have to see one person dealing humanly with another. They have to sense that you're more than a machine spewing information at them. Catechists have to try to engender more than openness to new information."

George caught the waitress's eye and signaled for more coffee. Roger meanwhile noticed for the first time how beautiful the Christmas decorations looked up and down Windsor Avenue.

"You know my immortal words, don't you, George? If it's not personal, your catechizing won't count for much. We have to know those adolescent boys and girls as well as we can, their home situations, their desires and fears, their hopes, their thoughts and feelings about Jesus and Christianity.

"The more we know them, the better we can relate to them and make our classes more personal in tone. We can also fine-tune our teaching to their needs. We have to be careful about always answering questions they're not asking. When we're personal, then we are working with them as co-seekers for truth, for goodness, and for the Christ of faith."

George finished his coffee and observed, "I hear you saying that I need to be more balanced, that I should get to know the students personally, be open to their insights and questions, and care about their growth in faith."

Roger nodded. "And you don't have to be chummy to do this. You just have to be yourself." He looked out again at the Christmas decorations. "It's like Christmas. If that wasn't personal, it was nothing. God couldn't have been more personal than by becoming one of us, caring for us and abiding with us." As he listened to Roger, George remembered a Christmas verse he had stored two decades earlier:

From the very start
he is one with you.
Burden-bent and laden down with struggle,
he extends his gentle arms to embrace
your tear-stained lives.

"Now that's being personal," he thought.

He asked for the check and thanked Roger for his help. "But I'm still going to consider my decision. What you've said about being personal makes sense, but I'm not sure this is for me. Maybe by the end of the school year, I'll feel better about teaching. We'll see."

The two catechists stepped into the cold night and walked under the Christmas decorations in different directions.

*F*or *R*eflection and *D*iscussion

1. How would you assess and characterize your relationship to your class and to individuals in it?

2. How might you grow in knowledge of your students?

3. How would you distinguish between a personal and impersonal tone in your class? What is the difference be-

tween being "chummy" with your students, and being "personal"?

4. Do you view your students as co-seekers of truth with you?

5. If you are considering resigning as a catechist, have you analyzed the idea honestly and considered the causes of your feelings?

*P*RAYER

God, you have called me to teach others about you. Mindful of your gracious presence among us, may I see you in my students and be aware that they can also teach me about you. Amen.

6

LESLIE CREWS

From then on, Jesus began to make it clear to his disciples that he was destined to go to Jerusalem and suffer grievously at the hands of the elders and chief priests and scribes and to be put to death and to be raised up on the third day.   —*Matthew 16:21–27*

LESLIE CREWS sat at her kitchen table with a pencil in her hand, but it wasn't moving. She kept rereading what she had written. "New Catechetical Year Begins—Seventh and Eighth Grade Catechists Sought." It wasn't much, only a title, but at least the first words were on paper, which she had always considered the hardest part of any writing. At such a time she always recalled a quip by a writer: "Writing is easy. All you do is sit down at your typewriter (your kitchen table?) and open up a vein."

Her assignment, which typically was difficult in coming to birth, was to write an article for the deanery newsletter on recruiting junior high catechists. As the director told her, the assignment was hers because she was the "veteran" junior high catechist in the deanery—"Only four years makes me a veteran?" Leslie remembered asking herself—and because she had somehow developed a reputation for being able to put one sentence after another.

Leslie was never really excited about a writing assignment, but she did like teaching at Saint Isidore. Like many other catechists, she got into the work without much enthusiasm. Once, she would have said "unwittingly." But after four years she had learned a good deal about catechetics, about the teaching of the church, and about herself. She had grown in confidence and, more important, in knowledge of early teenagers and in her liking for them. Leslie wanted to continue as a catechist, and would not trade the grade level for any other. She stared at the refrigerator and thought, "On balance, the growth I've seen in the kids and the generally pleasant relationship I've had with them have greatly outweighed the unpleasant and discouraging experiences. It's really been worth it."

Leslie heard her husband's footsteps. She thought "the price" would be the theme of the newsletter article. "Linc, I've got it," she called out as she began to write. She wanted to share her discovery. Lincoln was already at the table. "What have you got? I was just coming in to pour some juice. Want some?" Leslie nodded as she began to explain. "Linc, this article I've got to write—the one on the need for junior high teachers?—I think I've got the approach. It may be obvious to those who are already into it, but I want to play up the challenge and the fact that the experience, the adventure, is really worthwhile."

Linc set a glass of juice in front of Leslie, who carried a questioning tone in her explanation. "I mean," she went on, "you know how I've come to appreciate my work as a catechist with those kids. You even joined us the times we've held our class sessions here. The discussions we had, their deep concerns and questions, their interest in Jesus...." Linc, who was now leaning against the doorpost, added, "and don't forget their enthusiasm. They're pretty emotional, but that can also work in their favor. We've seen their dedication in their service projects. Remember how they organized and managed the hunger walk last year?"

As Linc spoke, Leslie jotted a few phrases and then looked up. "That's the results, the rewards, of being a junior high catechist, but this recruiting article has to include 'the price' in order to show that it's worth the effort and time...."

"Yes, and the disappointments and annoyances. I almost said 'aggravation,'" Linc went on. "You have to admit, Leslie, that the sessions take a lot of planning, and you sometimes need a lot of patience and understanding during them. You've complained to me more than once about what it demands of you." Leslie was nodding as Linc quickly added, "That's the price you're paying, and you go right on paying it. You evidently think it's worth it!"

"Right. And this is what I want to say in the newsletter. I want people to have their eyes wide open when they consider being a junior high catechist. I want them to know the satisfaction and the joy in it...and what it'll cost them. I suppose it's a question of motive. When you want something enough, you pay the price." Leslie got up and walked over to the sink with her glass. She leaned against the counter and continued.

"I'm going to tie this all in with yesterday's Gospel reading. It makes the same point we're talking about, doesn't it?" Linc didn't want to admit he didn't recall it, so he waited for Leslie to go on. "Jesus felt something was eminently worthwhile; he had a motive. He 'had to' go up to Jerusalem, to the terrible events that awaited him there. And the Scripture people see this in Luke, drawn out over several chapters, as a kind of dramatic journey to Jerusalem and the passion and resurrection. Jesus set his face toward Jerusalem, as the Gospel tells it, and wouldn't turn away from it. It's a question of knowing the goal you want, and heading toward it, whatever the cost."

By this time Linc had recalled the Gospel reading at the Eucharist the day before. "More than that, Les. There's also that invitation to take up the cross if we want to be Jesus' disciples. That's another case of paying the price if something is really worthwhile. You've got the right message for the junior high teachers. Start with the Gospel picture of Jesus setting his face toward Jerusalem. Then be very clear about the price of being a catechist, and conclude with the benefits, the accomplishments."

Leslie went over to the table again as Linc asked, "Want to call it a day and go up?" Leslie kept on writing. "I'll be up shortly. I have to get these thoughts on paper."

As Linc was leaving, he turned to say, "You should really speak to prospective catechists in person, Les. Then they couldn't helping catching your enthusiasm."

For Reflection and Discussion

1. What is your enthusiasm level as a catechist?
2. How would you rate the enthusiasm of your students? To what would you attribute this? How could you increase it?

3. How would you describe the "price" you pay to be a good catechist? Why are you willing to pay this price?

4. Above all else, what do you want to achieve this year as a catechist?

5. If you had to write an article to recruit catechists for your grade level, what would you say?

PRAYER

How I wish I felt more enthusiastic about my work as a catechist. And yet, God, I am faithful to this calling; I work hard at it; I care so much about those I teach and the way I teach. This is what I should keep in mind, by your grace: it is what I do as a catechist that counts, not how I feel. Amen.

7

John Pimentel

Then Peter spoke to Jesus. "Rabbi," he said, "it is wonderful for us to be here." —Mark 9:2–10

JOHN PIMENTEL wondered how long the brash rock music would overpower the catechists' prayer meeting. He looked up understandingly as his host excused himself from his guests and walked sternly up the stairs to the second floor bedrooms. Instantly, there was silence. "I've seldom heard silence so sweet," John mused.

After a moment, one of the other catechists volunteered, "We used silence during our prayer this evening, but we never spoke about it directly at all. It seems to me that we take for granted the important role of silence in our prayer." Another catechist added, "In class too. Teaching prayer in class is bound up with our own views on prayer and with our prayer habits. How should we use silence in class? Do we make use of it?"

"Or are we afraid of it in class?" John found himself saying to the group. He was surprised at this because he had never thought about silence in this way. He only wished that this subject had come up earlier in the evening.

By this time the host had returned to his seat with a look of embarrassment on his face. After some final remarks, the meeting broke up and the catechists stood around in small groups, chatting and having a snack. John was curious, as he sugared his coffee, to listen to his peers talking about silence. At first, it was about poor Steven's embarrassment with his kid's music, then it was the impact of the silence following, and finally the importance of silence for prayer. "A rare and precious commodity in our society," John chipped in, "something we better try to cultivate and appreciate."

His peers around the dining room table were listening as John went on. "Think about it. A 15-second pause for reflection at Mass makes us think the celebrant lost his place. We can't wait on the phone or ride an elevator without music being pumped at us. Many kids won't walk down the street or skate in the park without a walkman. Words in conversation or on the radio fill up our day. Phones are ringing, motors are humming, horns are blowing. People even turn on the television just so they won't be uncomfortable with the silence or alone with their thoughts."

Maggie, the middle-grade coordinator, came closer to the point as two more catechists joined the group. "Somewhere in our frenzied lives we have to make occasional room for positive silence, moments however brief and sporadic, to let serenity sink into our souls. How good this would be for our mental well-being and for our composure and self-awareness."

"And, of course, for our prayer," Steven interrupted. "It may depend on what you think prayer is, but it seems to me you can scarcely pray without a chance to be alone with your thoughts and feelings from time to time. This silence is not just for the moment of prayer itself; it's just as much for what I'd call a preliminary to prayer: a moment of self-awareness. It's a time to say to ourselves, 'Look. Here you are, in these circumstances, with these feelings, with this agenda, and with these thoughts. Relish the moment—or at least be aware of it!' And it may be no more than a moment. We have to become more sensitive to the opportunity and value it in our busy lives. As I see it, that's an important condition for prayer."

"Like spiritualizing the moment," John suggested.

"Or, of course," Maggie contributed, "being open to the Spirit. It's a kind of creative listening, isn't it? This moment of silence may be just being aware of the Spirit, a quiet awareness of God's presence."

Hearing this, Steven was anxious to make a point. "Then this brief time of silence I spoke about before as a preliminary to prayer may in fact be prayer itself, a momentary awareness in one's whole person of being in the presence of God."

Some catechists by the front door called out that they were leaving and John waved goodbye. "Steven's point just now," he said, "is exactly the image Deacon Murkheim described yesterday in the homily. At the transfiguration, Peter made the suggestion to build shelters so that they could stay there on Mount Tabor to absorb and relish the experience with Jesus. 'How good it is for us to be here,' Peter said. I guess that's how we should feel about those periods of silence that may become interludes of prayer."

He looked at the wall clock and asked to be excused. As

he was putting on his parka, he said to Maggie and Steven, "What we never got to was prayer for our students, prayer in class, silence in their lives and its connection with being aware of God's presence, even momentarily."

John thanked his host, then turned to the group and said, "We should really talk more about this....Good night, and thanks."

Outside he pulled up his high fur collar and leaned against the biting wind as he made his way to the car. After he started the engine, he turned on the radio and waited for the engine to warm up. He sat back and stared at the ice crystals on the windshield as he thought about the discussion on silence and how it might lead to prayer. "I really have to think a lot more about prayer and the kids I teach... and about silence in their lives." Then, as if someone had tapped him on the shoulder, John realized what he had done. He shook his head as he reached over to turn off the radio. As he started down the street, he felt enveloped in a warm and soothing silence. "How good it is for us to be here," he said to himself.

For Reflection and Discussion

1. What do you think about silence in your life? What place does it have in daily life?

2. Do you try to cultivate periods of silence on a regular basis?

3. Examine your thoughts about the relationship between silence and prayer.

4. In class, do you purposely use silence, including your own, for any reason? What are some examples?

5. Do you and the students pray in class? Do you use silence effectively for this purpose?

PRAYER

I am in your presence, God, now and always. Help me to embrace moments of silence, I ask you, so that I may be steeped in a deep awareness that you are with me and with those I teach. May we learn to embrace occasional silence to find you—and ourselves—more readily. Amen.

8

HECTOR ACEVEDO

Seeing the crowds, he went to the mountain. And when he was seated his disciples came to him. This is what he taught them: How blessed are the poor in spirit; the kingdom of heaven is theirs. —Matthew 5:3–12

HECTOR ACEVEDO stretched easily as he rose from the armchair at the end of the meeting and went over to the refreshments. He was happy to meet each month with the other middle-grade teachers to work on lesson plans, to discuss common problems, and to exchange ideas on recent readings. The gatherings in each one's home were usually very helpful, but the exercises or discussions always made him feel a little self-conscious. Because he was the senior member of the group, aside from the DRE, the others looked to him for opinions. He didn't feel he deserved this unofficial position. Still, the topic this October evening was just what he wanted. After four years of teaching fourth graders, he welcomed the opportunity to develop some fresh approaches to teaching morality, something beyond what his teacher's manual offered.

As Hector poured himself a cup of coffee, he overheard Larry and Marjorie talking about the place of the beatitudes in the fourth-grade curriculum. The subject interested him and he thought he might learn something from his associates. He turned to join them, putting aside the temptation to mention that ecology is now being suggested as a basis, or norm, of morality.

"But you don't have to base a course in morality on the beatitudes," Marjorie was saying, "...or the Ten Commandments for that matter."

"I know, Marjorie; but both those topics merit more than a passing interest," Larry replied. "Our long tradition alone grants them more than that. He turned to include Hector in the conversation. "What do you think, Hector?"

"About the beatitudes? They're here to stay," Hector quipped. "Seriously, from what I've heard, you two should do some research to see how much the beatitudes are used in moral teaching and what function they have. For a start, just go through all the catechetical programs at the parish center. Which ones base their approach on the beatitudes or use them in a substantial way, or just mention them in passing?"

"Sharing the Light of Faith does," Marjorie suggested.

"The directory. Good," Hector said. "You know, there's no doubt, according to the directory, that the beatitudes should be included in moral catechesis; it's one of the accepted methodologies. Let's see, I think it says they can be used for presenting values, qualities to be cultivated. Even that the specifics of morality can be taught through them. The beatitudes definitely have something to add to our courses, but I doubt that anyone would recommend using them exclusively."

"You know, I've heard them referred to as...the spiritual charter of the kingdom," Larry offered. "They're really rich and I think they're overlooked as a whole."

"Or overworked?" Marjorie retorted. "They may be rich, but they are pretty complicated. There's a lot of writing about the precise meaning of each one. There's a question whether they're required behavior for the reign of God, extreme demands, or unachievable ideals that we're to aim at."

Hector sipped his coffee and said, "I'm sure there's some truth in each of those last descriptions, and none is entirely true. I think they're very useful and, yes, rich in their own way. As with the Ten Commandments, there's a way to understand them in their context and original meaning, and a way to legitimately understand them and use them today."

Larry asked for an example as Bill Holleran joined the group.

"Well," Hector went on, "when I heard the Gospel read last year at the school Mass on All Saints Day, I made a connection between the beatitudes and saints; you know, the sainthood we can all achieve, not just the canonized kind. What did somebody call it? 'A saint is a person grasped by a religious vision that is so central to life that it radically changes the person.' This may be the same thing, but I like to think of a saint as someone imbued with the awareness of God's presence. It is more than ordinary sensitivity to the fact that God stands within and all about. And it's not the 'God is watching' kind of awareness."

Larry pressed for the connection with the beatitudes.

"I'm almost there," Hector assured them. "I think of the

beatitudes as expressions of the saint's basic posture or attitude before God, in whose presence the saint is so conscious of standing. No matter what meaning you give to each of the beatitudes, you see it as a particular posture before God.

"For example"—Hector put his cup down—"the beatitude about 'purity of heart' is presented with different meanings, but let's take it as total integrity and commitment to God, more than purity of thought and deed. However the beatitude is interpreted, it is presented as a fundamental way we stand in God's presence."

Marjorie added, "A concrete expression of our relationship to God."

Hector nodded and continued, "Think of all the beatitudes as expressions of our awareness of God's presence: the 'poor in spirit' as the social outcast, the desperate; the 'merciful' as those who pardon and are open to the guilty; the peacemaker as a healer in all areas of society. I think we have to do more than explain each beatitude; we have to teach an attitude about them. This attitude is that they are all expressions of our posture before God, of our awareness that we stand in God's presence. This awareness can make saints of us all. Marjorie glanced at her watch. "I've enjoyed your insights, Hector, and I hate to go now, but I like to kiss my kids good night."

Hector nodded. "What a nice reason to have to leave. I know it's getting late. One thing though: The attitude I'm talking about, of being aware of God's presence, is good to use in teaching the beatitudes, but it's an important attitude for every topic we cover."

Hector paused a moment as the group started to break up. "I know it's corny, but remember: be-attitude."

FOR REFLECTION AND DISCUSSION

1. How would you describe the beatitudes? Have you tried to understand them better by reading a commentary?
2. How would you describe a saint? How would you present the concept in class?
3. How would you link holiness to the beatitudes?
4. If you formally teach morality in class, what role do the beatitudes play in your presentation, even if your textbook doesn't make much mention of them?

PRAYER

My basic attitude in all of life is that you, God, are always present. I pray that this awareness may deepen ever more, and that it may profoundly affect the catechizing I do in your name. Amen.

9

MARYANN BROUDER

If anyone wants to have your shirt, give your coat as well. And if anyone asks you to go one mile, go an extra mile with that person. —Matthew 5:38–42

Maryann Brouder stepped into her apartment late one mild January evening, laid her attaché case on the table, hung up her coat, and put the kettle on the stove for tea. On her way home from her meeting with confirmation parents she remembered with a sting the talk she had to prepare for Sunday's gathering. The quarterly conference with the parish catechists was only three days off. When she began as the parish DRE, she initiated the practice of having the staff get together regularly to talk over common problems, to hear a speaker, to pray—and to enjoy one another's company. She always reserved minutes at the end for a pep talk and some praise. Her experience in catechetics had convinced her that beyond their training and even certification, catechists need words of appreciation and exhortation very much—in regular doses.

As Maryann poured a cup of tea, she thought it a paradox that on the one hand catechists had to be praised for their hard work, and, on the other, had to be exhorted to work harder. They needed to be supported with praise and shown appreciation for what they did week after week and in some cases year after year. She knew from her experience as a full-time teacher how trying and even exasperating the work can be. She was aware of the importance of motivating the catechists to sustain them in the enterprise. Love of the kids, self-fulfillment, participation in the ministry of the church—these would have to keep them going, doing the right work for the right reasons. "There isn't much else to offer them," she thought.

She carried the tea back to her easy chair and stood by it for a moment, looking out over the slushy street. The two sides of the paradox clashed in her mind. She sipped some tea and sat down. How odd, she thought, that with all the encouragement and support that catechists needed for their hard work, it was still necessary to exhort them to work harder. She recalled one principal remarking, "Learn to work smarter, not harder." "True," Maryann replied to herself, "but working smarter is hard work in itself."

The clock struck eleven and Maryann settled back, her mind pursuing the paradox. As any school administrator knows, teachers work at different levels of intensity. Her catechists were much the same, even with their ministry motivation. Some worked harder than others and put in more hours of class preparation. Maryann felt the need to encourage (invite, entice, lure, exhort) the catechists to do what they had to in order to be more effective. Part of that might be working smarter. She hoped to get them thinking about their effectiveness, about their willingness to go beyond the comfortable, the adequate, and the merely sufficient performance of their ministry.

"The extra mile" came to Maryann's mind as she set her mug on the end table. She remembered the charter statements in the Sermon on the Mount: "If a person in authority makes you go one mile, go two miles." "If someone wants to have your shirt, give your coat too." And that series of invitations: "You have heard it said...but I say to you...." Maryann thought of all these statements from Matthew 5 and 6 as invitations to go beyond the minimal requirements of Christianity, to enter more fully into its spirit of serving.

Maryann's talk to the catechists was falling into place. Lent was only three weeks off and her theme would set the tone not only for the catechists themselves, but for them to use in their classes. They might use it at opportune times, in incidental teaching, to promote a positive attitude toward Lent. An "extra mile" lenten theme might set a tone not only for their own teaching, but for the children's observance of Lent.

When the clock struck again, Maryann realized she'd have to get into the details of her talk at some other time. But she found it difficult to still her active mind. She knew she'd have to offer the catechists suggestions on how they might work harder—or smarter. One of the clearest lessons she had ever learned from teaching was that whenever you have a good idea for better teaching, it also means more work. "A relentless axiom of pedagogics," she said to herself as she smiled.

Some examples of a catechist going the extra mile ran through Maryann's mind as she stood up and finished her tea, which had become cool: thoroughly previewing videotape presentations; reviewing written work completely, even adding useful comments and suggestions; going out of the way to learn what might lie behind a discipline problem; reading one more chapter or article to get a better grasp of the subject matter for a class; conferring with parents to get to know a student better; attending an optional workshop; praising a student's work when silence is easier; keeping full and accurate class records; allowing adequate time for both remote and proximate class preparation; evaluating classes; and perhaps keeping written records of their own failures and successes.

It became clear to Maryann that there would be more suggestions than she could use in her talk. She felt good that she could offer enough to make her point. It was ironic that she should again experience the force of the fact that any step to teach others better will always mean more work...for the teacher. Once, she thought of it only in terms of a teacher and her classroom students. Now, in her desire to praise her catechists' work and urge them at the same time to work harder, to go the extra mile, *she* had to work harder. "I just hope this talk will help the catechists personally and lead to better teaching," she said to herself. "And to a more positive outlook on Lent."

Maryann took her mug into the kitchen and placed it in the sink.

For Reflection and Discussion

1. Are you going the extra mile to be a more effective catechist? How?

2. Do you evaluate your teaching habits regularly to see if there is something more you could do for your students?

3. Has it been your experience that whenever you have a good idea for better teaching, it also means more work for you? Give an example.

4. Do you feel sufficiently encouraged in your work? Sufficiently challenged?

5. Before and during Lent, do you try to instill a positive attitude toward the season?

Prayer

You know, God, that I have only so much time each week to devote to teaching your children. Enflame my spirit so that I may use this opportunity well. Encourage me not to be afraid of working hard in your name, and if I also work "smarter" in your name, I thank you. Amen.

10

Alice Gutierrez

Filled with the Holy Spirit, Jesus left the Jordan and was led by the Spirit into the desert. —Luke 4:1–13

ALICE GUTIERREZ told herself—again—that it was easy to get into a rut during Lent. "Year after year, the same Scripture readings, the same weary clichés about the need for penance, ashes on the forehead, abstinence, daily prayer, the inevitability of Easter." She walked along the paved path that girded Goldman Pond in the frigid, early morning air, thinking how she had to push herself each spring to see Lent in a fresh, invigorating way.

"Those Lents when I was a young woman—I didn't make enough of them," she thought. "That's because I used to think Lent was supposed to do something for me, instead of seeing it as a graced season when I was supposed to do something for myself—reading, reflecting, discussing, praying, and doing for others."

Her thoughts presently turned to those in her religion

class whom she cared for deeply, as she had cared for every one of the children in her classes over the past eleven years. It was very important to her to help her students grow in appreciation of Lent. But rather than "teaching Lent" in her classes, she used incidental stories and personal anecdotes, brief readings, and an occasional "Did you know...?" These were the ways she tried to "bring home" the significance of Lent to her sixth graders.

So here she was again this year, reading and praying about Lent, trying to see more in it than before. She was looking for a fresh insight, an angle, a theme, a motive for herself. She knew this was more important, and more effective, than planning directly for her students. The excitement and occasional exhilaration generated by this form of preparation would, she was convinced, come out in her teaching.

Alice stepped to the edge of the path to let two joggers go by. Just last evening she had begun reading about Jesus' confrontation with Satan in the desert, the Gospel for the First Sunday of Lent. As she pored over the passage, the theme she'd use for Lent this year began to emerge. "Fidelity!" she realized. "What else could it be?"

The passage began with such strong emphasis on the Spirit: "Full of the Holy Spirit...he was led by the Spirit." And Jesus followed the Spirit's lead. Alice was taken with Jesus' faithfulness to his mission. He answered the Spirit's call despite severe obstacles and strong temptations.

Looking across the pond, Alice knew she would not actually use the word "fidelity" with her students, but over the weeks they would be impressed with the many ways this quality touches their lives. "When they think of Lent," she thought, "I want them to think of being true to themselves, to their word, to their obligations and vocation—as Jesus was."

At the beginning of his public ministry, Alice recalled, Jesus encountered Satan in three dramatic scenes that put his sense of mission, self-esteem, and self-identity to a severe test. Satan tried to seduce Jesus into being untrue to his mission, his father, and himself. Alice conjured the scenes as she walked.

In the first scene, the tempter suggests that Jesus, who had been fasting and was famished, turn stones into bread. He challenges Jesus to use his power for himself, apart from the work his father sent him to do. "One does not live by bread alone," Jesus responded.

In the second scene, the tempter offers Jesus lordship over the earth, with all the glory that goes with it. Jesus has merely to do homage to the devil. But this would mean being untrue to his father. He makes it clear that his mission is to see that his father's reign is established everywhere. Only his father shall be worshipped.

Jesus is challenged in the third scene to show the populace how important he is by throwing himself off the temple wall and having his angels save him, a sensational display of miraculous power in order to conform to popular ideas about the Messiah. Jesus will not seek to draw such vain attention to himself; it will not advance his mission nor please his father.

In each of these scenes, Alice remembered, Jesus is tempted to be unfaithful to his mission, to disobey his father, to be what he isn't. But he stood firm in his fidelity. He tolerated no deviation from this single-minded purpose.

Alice recalled the line from *Hamlet* that her uncle used to quote: "This, above all, to thine own self be true."

The sun rose above the tall spruces across the pond and Alice continued her walk, now at a brisker pace. She would have to continue her planning that evening. There was, of course, the important matter of how this topic would be applied to the concerns and interests of her students, to their daily lives. "How much of life," she reflected, "comes down to keeping our word, being true to our promises, living up to our obligations, keeping faith with our calling." She knew the matter of fidelity would touch their lives deeply, and would even have impact on them in their early teens. "My occasional stories and comments in classes this Lent will touch them, I pray God...." Recalling that the passage in Luke began: "Filled with the Holy Spirit," Alice reminded herself that this would happen to her and her class only if they were open to the Spirit.

Alice looked forward to joining her husband for breakfast as she left pondside and headed for home three blocks away.

For Reflection and Discussion

1. Have you thought about a lenten theme for yourself? What will it be?

2. Do you, like Alice, spend time reflecting on an overall theme for your lenten classes?

3. Are you aware of the impact of your stories, anecdotes, and examples?

4. Do you read the lenten Gospels as background for your weekly lessons?

5. What do you think about arranging to meet with other catechists to discuss a lenten theme?

PRAYER

What am I as a catechist, God, unless I am faithful to you, to your word that I proclaim, to your call, to your children whom I teach? Let me be led by your Spirit so that, filled with a passion for fidelity, I may always be your faithful catechist. Amen.

11

SANDRA LEFFINGWELL

After John had been arrested, Jesus went into Galilee. There he proclaimed the Gospel from God saying, "The time is fulfilled, and the kingdom of God is close at hand." —Mark 1:14–15

SANDRA LEFFINGWELL stood at her living room window and waved to her son. He was rushing down the snow-packed street to catch the school bus, his books askew under his arm and his jacket half on. He was late again and didn't notice her waving. Anyway, she thought, he's too old for this ritual, which we've been doing for too long.

With the house quiet again, she poured a second cup of coffee and sat down with some notes she'd been writing during the week for the eight high school kids who'd be over that evening for their biweekly gathering. Lent was a week away, and Sandra had first begun some years earlier to try to make something of Lent for her students. She was acutely interested in teaching them about the season and in motivating them to make it a time of renewal and reevaluation, a time of slowly developing their self-awareness of their relationship to God and the others in their lives. Each year Sandra refined her approach to Lent and became more realistic as she grew to appreciate high schoolers: their activities, their interests and inclinations, their capabilities and idealism.

A new high school catechist, Caitlin Wetherfield, who was coming over that evening as an observer, was also dropping by this morning to prepare the session with Sandra. She was especially interested in seeing how Sandra handled Lent with the students and used a particular theme for the season.

Sandra felt she was obliged to make something of Lent each year; no question. Her own prayer-filled reflection on its meaning and utter usefulness had shown her that it was "good news" to share with her family and students. She had been moved—deeply affected—by her consideration of the great themes usually associated with Lent: renewal, reform, repentance, commitment, covenant.

But Sandra had also learned (from her earlier students) an application of the "more is less" principle. Instead of letting her enthusiasm for the benefits of lenten considerations mislead her into doing and saying too much in her classes, she had found that after an introduction to Lent and a related theme it was more effective to touch on the subject briefly or only obliquely in each class. In this way, she felt, she could keep the subject alive and motivate the students by occasional offhand observations and questions. If a discussion arose from her planned "incidental remarks," she didn't discourage it.

Poring over her scribbled notes, Sandra recalled her decision to make "kingdom" the theme of her lenten classes this year. She thought this would give the students a sense of being part of the kingdom. It would help them realize that they are to build up God's reign, that each one can make it more actual and present. She thought she would tell them of Louis Evely's observation that "God has no one but us to do the very things we ask for." In other words, she told herself, we're all God's got.

The doorbell rang. "Good morning, Caitlin," Sandra said as she stepped aside to let her in. "I'll get you some coffee." Caitlin sat down and noticed Sandra's notes. "I see you're going with kingdom as your theme."

"Yes. I thought the Sunday Gospel next week gives us the direction we need: 'Repent and believe; the kingdom of God is at hand.' We should try to make this kingdom a reality in the kids' lives, at least so that it can begin to be part of their decisions."

Sandra served Caitlin the coffee and sat down. "But selecting a lenten theme is not enough to talk about. 'Kingdom' is broad, really vague. You have to get an angle on it and show the kids what it means to them and how it should affect them, what they can do about it."

"In other words," Caitlin cut in, "make it visible and tangible, something they will care about."

Sandra picked up on Caitlin's comment. "That's the key right there. You have to move the kids and touch their feelings; you have to motivate them so that they not only want to learn more, but want to *do* something—in this case, about the reign of God." Caitlin's expression asked the obvious question. Sandra read it and said, "What's the 'kingdom' angle, right? I was thinking of justice and peace. It's in the air these days: articles, conversations, homilies. One of the best connections between kingdom and justice I ever heard was last October, Father Sadowski's homily on Christ the King. He developed the liturgy's words, 'a kingdom of justice and peace.'"

Caitlin pushed her cup aside as she said, "The connection is clear enough when you think about it: building the kingdom of God and working for peace and justice." She started to write some notes and went on, "How will you interest the kids? Their ideas on justice can be pretty narrow."

I was thinking of people's needs, the more obvious ones such as hunger and shelter...there are so many; you hear about them all the time, especially when you've become more sensitive to the great number of people around the world who don't have what we can so easily take for granted: clothing, housing, food, jobs, freedom."

Sandra took some newspaper and magazine clippings from a folder. "I think it would be good to spend some time on factual items like these, limiting ourselves just to hunger. One clipping here says 15 million people die each year from hunger-related causes. And hunger is not only in Chad or Pakistan; it's right here too, the Bentley Street Soup Kitchen, for example."

Sandra gestured to make a point. "I want to interest the kids in a project connected with hunger. I've heard of some high school people working on some imaginative and really useful projects to help the hungry. There are even hunger retreats. There has to be some amount of doing to go along with the sensitizing we're trying to accomplish. One drives home the other."

The phone rang and Caitlin read one of the clippings until Sandra came back to sit down. "That was the school," Sandra said matter-of-factly. "They wanted to let me know that Jimmy was late again. He missed the bus and had to walk to school." She and Caitlin shook their heads, smiling. Then she said, "Let's see what we can do with 'kingdom and justice' in our sessions this Lent."

For Reflection and Discussion

1. What attention do you give to educating your students about Lent?

2. How do you view Lent yourself? Where does it fit in your spirituality?

3. Consider having your students do something during Lent, perhaps something to assist others. What might such a project be?

4. Do you share lesson preparation with other catechists, at least for special occasions or projects? Why or why not?

5. Are you growing to know your students better? Are you gradually adapting your lessons to their abilities, interests, backgrounds?

Prayer

As I teach, God, grace me with an ever deeper awareness of the dire needs of others around the world and down the street. Help me to move beyond the words of my teaching to work for those in need. Inspire me, God, to broaden the world of the boys and girls in my care. Amen.

12

RICHARD TORTELLI

And it happened that, as [Jesus] was praying, the aspect of his face was changed and his clothing became sparkling white. —Luke 9:28–36

RICHARD TORTELLI stepped out of his house into the bright February sunshine, his bowsaw in hand. It was one of those perfect days he would see only a handful of times a year, a day that would draw him into some precious moments of self-awareness, reflection, and prayer. He would experience a heightened consciousness of God as he drew his saw back and forth on a tall maple sapling. At times he would raise his eyes past the wavering stark limbs to the rich blue sky, breathe deeply, and inhale the presence of God.

In the utter brilliance of this cold winter morning the image of Jesus' transfiguration—Jesus' face "brilliant as the sun"—came to Richard's mind. Squinting at the icy-blue sky, he thought about that pivotal, revealing, and hope-engendering moment.

As Luke describes it, the wondrous change in Jesus' appearance before the eyes of Peter, James, and John signals a turning point in his life. Shortly before this event, Herod, hearing about all that Jesus was doing, asked "Who is this man?"

Then Jesus himself asked Peter, "Who do you say I am?" and Peter answered, "You are God's Messiah." Jesus then announced his own rejection and execution, and described the ultimate, heavy cost of discipleship.

After his transfiguration, Jesus would undertake his prolonged journey to Jerusalem where he would rendezvous with Calvary. But now, on this mountain with his friends, the "glory" of God momentarily shines through.

This awesome moment was also deep revelation, Richard thought as he admired again the glory of the winter day. Clearly echoing the Father at Jesus' baptism, a heavenly voice proclaims Jesus as son and chosen one. What words could say more about his essential character, his very being? Richard wondered. In Jesus' case, to be son is everything; not to be son is to be nothing.

The glory Jesus manifested at this transfiguration, which he included in the prediction of his passion, would also be a part of the destiny of his followers, Richard thought. Their journey to Calvary would end with Easter because of their relationship with Jesus. On the Mount of Transfiguration Jesus gives us all hope. His glory manifested is a pledge of our own glory.

As Richard stood back to watch the maple sapling fall, his thoughts were still on human destiny. He was just glad there was a God-filled life of joy and peace, even though he had to admit that he sometimes tried in vain to "picture" it. The image of the glory that awaits us, hinted at in the transfiguration, would have to suffice to support him. In fact, he knew deep down that amid the trials of life he'd have to cling to the barest image of it with the tightest grip he could manage. "A man's reach must exceed his grasp, or what's a heaven for?" he recalled as he dragged the slim trunk to a clearing. "Somewhere there's something beautiful waiting for me."

Richard thought of his catechetical work the past four years. It had been very satisfying. He was working hard to make the faith of the boys and girls "living, conscious, and active." When he could see beyond the troublesome details and annoyances, his teaching was essentially exciting and gratifying, a part of a great adventure. He felt rewarded too because he continued to grow in knowledge, love, and faith.

"But," Richard thought as he stacked the timber, "it's a mixed bag; teaching religion can also be quite unsatisfying." The good results he hoped, prayed, and worked for were often unknown to him in any detail. He would seldom have the satisfaction of seeing results. He could only believe that his efforts would produce good fruit through the Holy Spirit.

Richard recalled the maxim, "Pray as if all depended on God, but work as if all depended on yourself." As he headed toward another stand of trees to thin it out, he smiled. "It's probably a good thing that I don't get to see all the results of my efforts!"

*F*OR *R*EFLECTION AND *D*ISCUSSION

1. How does the maxim about prayer and work apply to you as a catechist? Do you work hard and pray hard to be an effective tool of God?

2. Why, in the end, might Richard be just as glad not to know the results of his catechizing?

3. Do you ever consider how your catechizing might affect the future of your students? Are you concerned only with the next day or the next week?

4. In what specific ways can your work as a catechist help you to grow?

PRAYER

I have no choice, God, but to trust you with the results of my teaching. I leave in your hands what may come of my ministry of proclaiming your word. Grant me the wisdom to be concerned only with working hard in your name and by your grace. Amen.

13

Teresita Munoz

Whoever drinks this water will be thirsty again; but no one who drinks the water that I shall give will ever be thirsty again: the water that I shall give will become a spring of water within, welling up for eternal life.
—John 4:5–42

TERESITA MUNOZ stopped at the barrio well, surprised to see no one drawing water. There was only a woman struggling down the clay road with a yoke across her shoulders, balancing on each side a two-gallon tin of water. Teresita got out of her Jeep and fondly tapped the hood, as if to thank the old machine for safely completing another trip over the rough roads. As she pumped a cup of water, she felt gratified at the progress the catechists were making at San Miguel Church. Each month she could see their enthusiasm and confidence growing. "That's more important than anything else," she thought.

Teresita hung the water cup by the spigot and turned toward her car when she saw one of the high school students, Milagros San Vicente, coming down the street with a water tin. "Milagros," she said as the slight girl approached, "it's good to see you. It must be three or four weeks." Milagros smiled tentatively and placed the tin under the spigot. "Yes, I'm sorry, Señora Munoz." After a moment she added, "My mother has been sick and I have to do the chores and take care of my brother and sister."

"Don't worry about it, Milagros. It's good of you to help her," Teresita said graciously, recalling that she had seen the mother regularly at the market looking rather well. She went on as Milagros pumped water into her tin, "I should have been by to see you, but with my visits to the catechists in the other barrios, I haven't had the time. Anyway, even though you've missed some classes, what do you think of the high school religious instruction at Cristo Rey Church? ...You can be open with me."

Milagros continued pumping and didn't look up. "I don't know, Señora Munoz; it's all right, but sometimes I really wonder why I should go. What we learn doesn't seem to matter so much to me. When I go to class or do an assignment, I dislike it more than math. I'm not even sure why."

"It must seem like a big waste of time to you." Milagros looked directly at Teresita for the first time and nodded. Teresita continued, "That's too bad, but I understand your feelings. Who likes to do something and not really know why they're doing it?" There was a brief pause. "Tell me, Milagros, is it the teacher that's the problem, or is it what you study? Why do you suppose there's so little interest?"

Milagros shrugged her shoulders. "I don't think Señor Alegre is the problem. He's like other catechists I've had. He tries hard and I think he's fair, but when he talks about Scripture, which we're studying now, I just daydream, write a letter, or do an assignment. Most of the time, I think,

I'm not even there. If I am there, my mind and heart aren't."

Teresita asked if her friends felt the same way. "And how," Milagros replied, as she finished pumping and turned toward Teresita. "Some of them go because their parents really make them, but most would rather be someplace else. I just think there's so much else they'd rather be doing and they resent being there."

"But don't they want to know more about God?" Teresita asked, realizing at once how naive the question was. Milagros replied that it wasn't because they didn't care about God. "But we're not learning anything new, and besides, most of us go to Mass pretty regularly. Some of us even made that retreat day a few months ago."

"Yes, that was really good," Teresita said, as they sat down on a bench by the well. "But, you know, you might consider joining the group again. You might find it worth your time. For one thing, we're going to have our gatherings in some of the catechists' homes. And we're going to try to tie the subject matter very closely to your lives and interests. More than anything, though, we don't want you all to think there's nothing else to know about God, about the Gospels, about the church and faith. What you and I don't know about God and these subjects could fill volumes. And the funny thing about this is that you can become infected with knowing Jesus. The more you know about Jesus, the more you want to know him, what he was like, how he is present in our world today."

Milagros looked intently at Teresita, who went on, "It's sad and I suppose it's happened for a number of reasons, but many of you have a bad taste in your mouths about religious instructions. We've mistaught you or you've forgotten the main point of it all—meeting Jesus, knowing him better, loving him more, and living with his values. Instead of this, you've experienced a 'class' like other classes, other school subjects.

"We know our high school groups are hardly the only opportunity to meet Jesus and learn about him, but being part of the group can be so useful, a very good way to get into it. This is what we want, and we're trying to learn to do this better and better." The sun was slipping behind the hills, but Milagros was content to listen on, showing little reaction to Teresita's words.

"From what you've told me, Milagros, there's not much motivation to get into our group, and that's our fault. You deserve another chance to...well, to let Jesus win you over, to hear his invitation to learn about him and follow him. When Jesus met a woman by a well, he described himself as 'living water.' He invited us to drink this water, which is himself. He told us that if we do, we'll never be thirsty again. Can you imagine that, with us coming here so often to draw water from this well! We may not have motivated you the way we should have, Milagros, but it's what we're trying to do.

"The water that Jesus offers us, himself, is the water of eternal life. That's how he described it. Marvelous, isn't it? That fits right in with our Easter season when we celebrate Jesus' resurrection and our own victory over death. That's why we want to do what we can to help you and encourage you to meet Jesus and learn more about him."

Teresita got up, and Milagros right after her. It was dusk. As they walked over to the Jeep, Milagros said goodnight. Teresita put her hand on Milagros's shoulder and said, "Thanks for listening. I hope you'll think about all this, about what we're trying to do. The next time you come here to draw water, you'll have to remember what the woman said to Jesus, 'Give me that water, and then I shall not be thirsty.'"

Milagros nodded and bent over to pick up her heavy tin of water.

For Reflection and Discussion

1. Have you realistically assessed the state of apathy in your class? Do you face up to disinterest when you find it?

2. Do you try to see the students' interest level from their viewpoint? Do you ask for their frank opinions?

3. Do you speak to disinterested individuals about their attitude, and try to find out the reasons for it?

4. What motivation do you offer them? Does it ever resemble what Teresita said to Milagros about Jesus?

5. Do you consciously try to motivate your students by what you do, as well as by what you say?

Prayer

God, we all thirst to know you and Jesus whom you sent, but most often we are not aware of it. May I, by your grace, not only become more conscious of my need for your living water, but also grow in my desire to lead those I teach to the fountain of your love. Amen.

14

Len Skyros

> "Master, which is the greatest commandment of the Law?" Jesus said to him, "You must love the Lord your God with all your heart, with all your soul, and with all your mind. This is the greatest and the first commandment. The second resembles it: You must love your neighbor as yourself." —Matthew 22:34–40

LEN SKYROS stepped aboard the ferry, feeling annoyed that he should be so nervous about addressing his peers. It was not the first time he had done this, and he thought he should be above feeling like a fourth grader about to recite Whittier on Parents' Night. He knew he had prepared well enough and he was almost confident that he had something to say to the local catechists' cooperative. The youth ministers took turns speaking to fifteen high school catechists and other youth ministers in the parishes on the island.

It was too raw, the wind too brisk, to sit outside, so Len found a seat inside by a window looking out toward the hills west of the sound. He was looking in his briefcase for his notes when Irene Oroski sat down beside him.

"Hi, Len. I haven't seen you since our last quarterly meeting. How're you doing?"

"Not bad, Irene," Len replied, wanting to say he didn't relish this meeting because he was the speaker. "I'm the speaker today, Irene. I hope you're ready for it. To tell the truth, I hope I'm ready."

"You'll be fine. You're almost the senior member of our group, and your talk last year was really good."

He had found his notes and begun to review them when the ferry started to churn out of the slip. "What are you going to talk about?" Len looked at Irene with a straight face and said, "I really don't have the foggiest." She laughed. "Well, please don't ask me to talk in your place." "Don't worry," Len said. "Actually, my talk is very simple. No big insights or anything like that. Just a reminder, really, based on this Sunday's Gospel on the two commandments."

For courtesy's sake, Irene wanted to ask Len to go on, but she had to wait for the raucous ferry horn to stop blowing. "Simple Gospel. Simple message for your associates? What point do you make?"

Len shifted in his seat to face Irene more directly. "Only that if we are to love others as we love ourselves, we ought to consider what we'd want our teachers to be like if we were the students. How would we want to be treated? What would be fair, respectful, realistic? I'm going to propose that the group recall their school days, in religion class or others, and brainstorm what they liked and didn't like about their teachers, what they admired, what they found helpful, stimulating, or boring. If we can do that and recall what it was like as students, I'm suggesting, it may turn into a very useful review of how we're doing now as youth ministers."

Irene nodded and looked for a while past Len over the choppy water to the hills. "What you're doing, Len, is taking that second great commandment as another expression of the 'golden rule,' to do to others as we would wish them to do to us. It's really a good approach; I'll say that."

They fell silent again for a while. Then Irene said, "Well, everybody's got a Mr. Chips, I guess." Len didn't get the allusion, so Irene added, "He's a teacher in James Hilton's novel *Goodbye, Mr. Chips* who's admired and loved by his students over many years. You know, he represents that very good teacher who stands out in your memory better than any other. We've all had a teacher or two we should imitate as catechists or youth ministers: interesting, concerned about us as individuals, generous with their time, willing to admit they were wrong or didn't have all the answers, open to suggestions, perhaps even a bit off the wall...."

Irene's voice fell off as she noticed the grin on Len's face. "You know," Len said, "maybe you should give the talk this afternoon. But you're right. That's what I had in mind. You really got into this idea. I hope the others show half your enthusiasm." Irene assured him they'd enjoy it. "Everybody needs a good way to review their work, and your idea can be so effective."

Len appreciated Irene's encouragement. "This exercise also works along negative lines. Who doesn't remember with a lot of annoyance and regret the teacher who was too busy to be concerned about you, who had no control of a class or even of a lesson plan, who made unrealistic demands, who was too often abrupt, arrogant, or moody, or who showed so little enthusiasm for what he or she was teaching? This could be your negative Mr. Chips, I guess."

The ferry horn forced Len to wait several seconds. "I'm going to say a little bit about the other great commandment too: loving God with your whole being. I thought I'd add this by way of motivation. I think of it as the hallmark of the catechist, the one necessary quality of a true catechist. If you have all the qualities of Mr. Chips and don't have this love and dedication, you've got an essential flaw. You're really just a clanging cymbal."

Len could make out the island ferry slip in the distance now. Sr. Emilia would meet them there and drive them to the retreat house.

"I hadn't thought of this before," Len mentioned, "but I could paraphrase that last part of the Gospel. 'Everything in catechetics depends upon these two commandments: love of God and love of students.' That says it all." "Amen to that," Irene added.

By now they could hear the engine slowing down as the ferry made its way toward the slip. "Thanks for your interest, Irene. You've helped me clarify what I want to say. You'll have to tell me more about this Mr. Chips."

Len walked outside to the deck with Irene. He leaned on the railing and looked down at the broken water sliding along the hull, trying to recall who his Mr. Chips was and what teacher qualities he would recommend to his peers.

*F*OR *R*EFLECTION AND *D*ISCUSSION

1. Who is your Mr. Chips?

2. What were this person's outstanding qualities as a teacher? Do you have any of these qualities? How may you go about acquiring and developing them?

3. How would you describe your attitude toward your students? Can they sense your respect and love for them?

4. Is love of God a major force in your teaching? How?

PRAYER

God, grant me the courage and the wisdom to be open with myself and to see my strong and weak qualities as a catechist. May I, by your grace, strive to become a more effective minister of loving service to those in my care. Amen.

15

Larry Prentiss

He said to them, "Come after me and I will make you fishers of people." —Matthew 4:18–22

LARRY PRENTISS removed a book from the shelf in the catechists' library and scanned the contents for something on ministry. The lecture on ministry he had just come from was very good. In fact, the talk prompted him to look for something to read on it. He was in his fourth year of teaching eighth graders and was dissatisfied with the scant treatment in the textbook. It was, he reasoned, because of the rapid development on the subject. Since ministry was the subject lately of so much writing and discussion, perhaps a later edition of the catechetical program would have more to offer the kids. Larry took the book over to one of the four tables in the room and began reading a section that looked helpful. In a few moments he was taking notes.

Mike Texeira, the parish deacon, was passing by the library and saw Larry. He stopped in to say hello but Larry didn't notice at first. "Why don't you let it go for tonight, Larry." Larry looked up and smiled, but before he could say a word Mike asked, "Say, what did you think of the talk? Really provocative with all that history!"

Larry put up his hand to slow Mike down. "A fine talk, Mike. Actually, it's just what I need for my class, something to fill me in on the richness of the idea of ministry. There's so much for the kids to learn about it. Like so many of us, they limit ministry to what you, the pastor, and the associates do around here. If the kids are logical, they'll think they have to be ordained to have a ministry; they'll think they have to be clerics. Anyway, I want to get more information about all of this and make it a larger part of the class treatment of the church."

"You're right, Larry. We all have to do a lot of homework on this. That's why tonight's talk was so good. It's funny; when a subject is new or revived, a lot of confusion can set in, and with a topic like this, some nerves can be touched. It can get pretty emotional. It really disturbs some people that there is an official ministry that doesn't belong to priests alone. It's not what they grew up with. They'll even allow a few functions for us deacons, but not for the laity."

Larry nodded and invited Mike to sit down. As he did so, Jennifer Minello, a fifth-grade catechist, came in and made a sign that she didn't want to interrupt their conversation. She went over to the sacraments shelf and picked up a book.

Mike continued, "This Sunday I'm going to preach on ministry. With this talk tonight and all, the timing is just right for the subject. And, of course, the Gospel is perfect for it. It's the one from Matthew on calling the apostles: 'Come with me and I will make you fishers.'"

Larry interrupted, "In the sense that we're all called to be ministers?"

"No, not at all," Mike went on. "Look, do you have a few minutes? I'd like to see what you think about the outline I have." Larry nodded and Jennifer came over to them. "With sacraments as the subject for the year, I'd like to join you if you're talking about the ministry aspect of them," she said apologetically.

"The first point I'd make," Mike began, "is to distinguish between service and ministry. In themselves, both words seem to have the same meaning, but let's say that service is what we are all called by God to perform: to care for others, to love them, to serve them in any way our circumstances allow. In this we follow Jesus the healer, the teacher, the provider, the forgiver..."

"And the foot washer," Jennifer added.

"Right," Mike grinned. "But ministry goes beyond this, not in the sense of doing more for people, but in the sense that it is a formal kind of service, something officially recognized or properly authorized by church leaders, something done in the name of the parish or diocesan community."

Larry inserted a thought that all ministry is service, but not all service is ministry. "Ministry is what you have to qualify for to be approved," Jennifer suggested.

"So it seems," Mike went on. "As you'd expect, there's some disagreement about who's a minister and who isn't. Some people want to link ministry only to liturgy. In which case, the lector is a minister and the catechist isn't. But if you follow the 'recognition, authorization' position, the catechist is a minister also."

"Actually," Larry inserted, "for the person intent upon helping others, this distinction wouldn't be a primary concern, to say the least. Jennifer, as a dedicated catechist, how much does it matter to you?" She nodded in agreement.

Mike went on to mention the second distinction he'd

make in his homily. "I'd also want to bring out the difference between ordered ministry—what we have called ordained ministry in the past—and non-ordered. This is an easier distinction; no dispute here over who's received orders and who hasn't. The bishop, priest, and deacon are ordered or ordained. The many other ministers we have at Immaculate Heart are not: the ministers of the sick, of music, of hospitality, of the Word, of the bread and cup, and the catechists. Except for a special closing question, that's what I have in mind for the homily....What do you think?"

Larry and Jennifer nodded approval and Mike added, "You know, it seems to me that the kids you teach—about sacraments and church—should not miss the big picture when you talk about ministry. It's not the title or rank of the ministers that's important. What's important is serving others. And it's not the minister who's important, but the individual or the celebrating community who's being served. And it's not whether the work is done in the name of the parish or in one's own name, as long as it's done in the name of Jesus."

As Jennifer got up to replace the book on the shelf, Larry asked, "What's that closing question you're going to ask, Mike?"

"Oh that," Mike mused. "Well, I was thinking of asking the congregation—and all of us have to ponder this—to what particular form of ministry or service is Jesus calling you today? Up till now, how have you answered this call?"

Larry stayed at the table as Jennifer and Mike walked toward the door. "Good luck with the homily on Sunday, Mike," Larry said as he opened the book on ministry again.

FOR REFLECTION AND DISCUSSION

1. After reading this chapter, how would you describe the meaning of ministry?
2. Do you agree with the distinction made between service and ministry? Why? Why not?
3. As a catechist, do you consider your work in the parish to be a ministry?
4. What does your textbook offer on this subject? To what other resources can you turn? What books or articles would you recommend?
5. List those persons in your parish whom you would identify as ministers. In general, what people in your parish are engaged in service?
6. When Jesus called the apostles to be fishers, was he also speaking to you? In what way?

PRAYER

I am restless, God, to serve your children in this work to which you have called me. Flood my spirit with yours so that I may see your presence not only in them, but in my co-catechists. May we all be united more closely with you and one another. Amen.

16

GENEVIEVE CHANG

Jesus said to them, "Come and have breakfast." None of the disciples was bold enough to ask, "Who are you?" They knew quite well it was the Lord. —John 21:1–14

GENEVIEVE CHANG stared out the bus window, not really noticing the listless shoppers or the drab store windows. She was thoroughly upset about the way her class had just gone! On top of that, she was embarrassed about the curt way she had spoken to the bus driver, including her mechanical apology. And the raw March afternoon rain did not help her mood.

Although she had been discouraged before about being a catechist, it was never like this. "What's the use?" she thought. This year had started out, like the three before it, with anticipation, enthusiasm, and realistic expectations. Yet her classes were often disappointing—and trying.

Genevieve was distracted when the driver called out a transfer stop. She noticed it was raining harder. The question that had been forming imperceptibly in her mind for some time came to her in a rush. "Should I quit?" With only two classes to go, she realized that she had to decide very soon about next year and give the DRE sufficient notice.

It would be a difficult decision. "God knows," she thought, "I haven't been all I should be as a catechist, but I've worked hard at this, including those certification courses." She was not really confident she was a good catechist and she doubted she would be able to handle fourth graders for one more year. There had even been some uncomfortable discussions with parents. "A lot of trouble with little to show for it," she reflected. Genevieve felt like telling herself that it wasn't worth it, but she stopped short of that.

As the bus was passing County Park, she remembered the talk at the recent day of recollection. How easy it was to recall the main lines of the resurrection story, which she had always liked. There was a warmth and lightness to it, a tone of quiet joy, a sense of peace about it. It touched her deeply. Peter announcing that he was going fishing, the others inviting themselves to go with him. Working hard all night and catching nothing. At dawn, a stranger calling from the shore, "You haven't caught anything, have you?" Just what the weary men needed. And what's more, directions on how to do it better. John recognizing the stranger: "It is the Lord." Peter's headlong swim to shore. Breakfast on Lake Tiberias: a charcoal fire, fish, bread. Jesus' invitation to eat.

Genevieve felt the bumpy crossing at the railroad tracks as the point of the talk forced itself on her: the revelation of Jesus, a theme running through John's Gospel. This was the stated purpose of the Baptist. At Cana, Jesus revealed his glory. He did the same when he cured a blind man. At the Last Supper, he spoke of revealing his father. Finally, Jesus revealed himself as Lord after the resurrection. It was the overriding purpose of his life, to reveal himself and his father, and he did it one more time at the lakeshore.

This ongoing revelation to the disciples took place, it seemed to Genevieve, in spite of themselves. They were slow to learn. They were blind at times, and their hearts were not always receptive. There was even the matter of discipline. They missed the point on more than one occasion. Yet Jesus continued to work at revealing himself. The pentecostal Spirit of God would lead them to a faith awareness and commitment, a fuller revelation they didn't realize they were capable of.

Genevieve was beginning to understand; it was hitting home. As a catechist, she was sincere about revealing the Lord to the children in her class—through her storytelling and other activities, her reading of Scripture, her efforts to encourage discipline, her prayer, her witness. All her preparation as well was for this purpose.

But Genevieve was honest enough to admit her own shortcomings. She was not always as well prepared as she might have been. She was impatient and even unkind sometimes. Occasionally she was too mechanical in her lessons, not open enough to those graced moments that would come up from time to time. And yet—the irony all catechists must face—even when she was well prepared and things seemed to go well, some classes were very disappointing.

When she saw her stop coming up, Genevieve began to get her coat and books together, still reflecting on the difficult school year that was coming to an end. She saw the negative aspects very clearly: disturbances in class, disrespect, lack of student effort, and apathy, even from parents. But there were positive things too.

"I have revealed the Lord," she thought to herself as she

moved toward the exit door. "I have sometimes enabled the children to see Jesus present and active in their lives. I have guided them toward a more mature faith. I have helped them grow familiar with God through prayer in Jesus' name." She knew that she had often done these things. "This is what my catechist's work is all about," she decided.

Genevieve stepped off the bus, relieved that the rain had let up. She no longer felt so upset. She felt better after having sorted out her feelings and looked at both sides of the question. "Still," she said to herself as she headed up Willing Street, "I'll have to decide pretty soon."

For Reflection and Discussion

1. Do you sometimes evaluate your teaching effectiveness and your teaching methods?

2. Do you keep the main purpose of your teaching always in view? Do you restate this goal from time to time?

3. When you experience setbacks or become discouraged, what do you do? Do you discuss the matter with anyone?

4. Are you, like Genevieve, tempted to resign? Have you sorted out all the reasons for and against this move? Have you talked it over with another catechist or your DRE?

5. Do you see a relationship between revealing the Lord and your role as a catechist?

Prayer

Thanks to you, God, I have much to give as a catechist. Let me see some of the good you do through me, and not think only of my weaknesses. When I become discouraged, help me to remember that you can be revealed through me. Amen.

17

LAURIE McKENNA

The disciples were filled with joy at seeing the Lord, and he said to them again, "Peace be with you. As the Father sent me, so am I sending you."—John 20:19–31

LAURIE MCKENNA got out of her chair and lifted her bag strap to her shoulder. She smiled a pleasant goodbye and walked out of the DRE's office. At Jane Llewellyn's invitation, Laurie had come almost an hour ago to talk over what she had mentioned to Jane after class a week earlier, that she was thinking of not returning next year as a catechist. She was quite direct in stating that her inclination to resign was not because she was moving out of the parish, or because she had taken a job with conflicting hours, but because she was "not content" with her work in that ministry, as she had put it.

Laurie walked down the wide granite steps of the turn-of-the-century stone building and turned up Barrington Avenue toward the subway station. She didn't feel especially good about the meeting because Jane had tried to persuade her to stay on for a second year. But so much was said to encourage her to remain a catechist and become a better one that she had to consider it further. She knew deep down that the reason she gave the DRE did not seem cogent—she had probably heard it from many catechists before—but it was enough to put Laurie on the verge of resigning.

As Laurie turned the corner, she noticed storm clouds darkening the April sky. A moment later she felt raindrops on her face as she approached the subway stairs, glad to be escaping the squall-like winds that had arisen. Walking the long, tiled corridor to the change booth, she recalled with surprise and relief that the DRE had not urged her to stay on because catechists were "hard to get." Laurie always felt the phrase made catechists sound like a commodity (she could hear her grandmother describing butter as "hard to get" during World War II), and not as flesh and blood people called to God's work.

As Laurie waited for the train, she kept thinking of the two themes that seemed to summarize Jane Llewellyn's effort to have her reconsider resigning: peace and faith. "She was almost eloquent," Laurie thought; "that was because she was so sincere." Laurie was struck by Jane's ideas about being at peace with yourself in your work.

She had said that it's just like being at peace with yourself in all of life; it's something that comes only from within. Being at peace as a catechist comes from utter honesty with yourself. It comes from a sober acceptance of who you are, a realistic assessment of your background and talents, and perhaps especially of your expectations. Jane had also said that sometimes a catechist suffers from professional depression because her expectations are unrealistic, too demanding. She doesn't have the practical wisdom to realize that to be a good catechist takes compelling effort and long years. We don't put that achievement on, as we would a coat, during the catechists' ceremony of commissioning.

She stressed that being at peace comes with the awareness that there has been improvement, that you have grown in your knowledge of the subject and love of the students, in your teaching methods and communication skills. Being at peace comes from a growing awareness of your deepening relationship with God and of how your catechetical ministry contributes to your spirituality.

Laurie looked up as the train appeared out of the tunnel darkness. She recalled saying she was "not content" as a catechist. She knew this was what the DRE meant by not being at peace, but she wondered as she stepped into the grimy, graffitied subway car whether she had been honest with herself during this first year, whether her discontent came from unrealistic and unfair expectations of herself.

She sat down and looked up at the dreary ads above the windows, not really seeing or hearing anything. "Peace" was the image she had of Sunday's Gospel, Jesus standing suddenly before his fearful and disappointed disciples. "He could have told them a thing or two about realistic expectations, honesty, and self-acceptance," she said to herself. She thought of Thomas too, and the faith that Jesus required of him.

Laurie recalled the faith that Jane had spoken of in their meeting. She had used it in two ways, faith in yourself and faith in the Holy Spirit. The director had made it clear that this faith was more than the catechist's faith, her prayer, her spirituality. It had to do with her faith in the Spirit's activity in her catechetical work. The true, lasting, and only real spiritual growth will come through the Spirit. She has to work as well and as hard as she can, but she has to leave the benefits to the Spirit.

Laurie knew that the more important meaning of this is that she shouldn't be evaluating her work in merely human terms. Simply, she had to rely on the Spirit to speak to the hearts of her students through her human efforts. What's more, she had to believe that the Spirit would speak to her students even through her poor classes and her earnest mistakes. She had to do what she could to be the best instrument she could be, to try to help the students to be open to the Spirit's gentle movements and whisperings.

These two thoughts, peace and faith, clanged in Laurie's mind as the train rumbled through the black tunnel. When she noticed her stop coming, she got up to stand by the door. She believed this peace and faith were required for catechists to be effective ministers. Did she have these qualities, she wondered? Could she? She'd have to think all this through; she owed it to herself and the DRE.

Laurie felt she had the talent to be a catechist and the determination to work hard at it—this was not the issue. She had to ponder whether she had the faith that Jane spoke about and whether she could be at peace as a catechist. These words, "faith" and "peace," burdened her mind as she walked up the subway stairs into a pleasant, sunny spring afternoon.

*F*OR *R*EFLECTION AND *D*ISCUSSION

1. Have you been tempted to resign as a catechist? Have you analyzed the real reasons for this?

2. What are your expectations as a catechist? Are they realistic?

3. Are you at peace with your catechetical work? Why? Why not?

4. What do you perceive to be your role in the catechetical process? The Holy Spirit's role? How are these related?

5. Have you discussed these thoughts with another catechist or your DRE?

6. Why, in your opinion, is there a large turnover of catechists every year?

PRAYER

Grace me, God, with your peace. Help me to be realistic about myself as a catechist, to be clear about my talents and shortcomings. Help me, too, to find contentment as a catechist, knowing that I am doing your work—as well as I can. Grace me, too, with a deep and abiding faith in you. Amen.

18

CLAUDIA BERKOWSKI

John the Baptist said to the crowds who came out to be baptized by him…"Produce good fruits as evidence of your repentance." And the crowds asked him, "What then should we do?" —Luke 3:7–14

CLAUDIA BERKOWSKI hung up the phone, feeling a bit annoyed. She was always glad to fill in as a substitute catechist at St. Anthony's, but here she was again with only a day to prepare the class. She could clearly recall the time she told Mr. Sammon she would be willing to help out from time to time, even though she could no longer be a full-time catechist. "Don't you be concerned," he had told her then. "I know how important it is to prepare class well. I'll always give you a few days' notice."

"I'm sure he meant well," Claudia allowed as she went to her desk to see what Lesson 14 was about. She sat down with her sixth-grade manual and turned the pages with interest. When she saw the lesson title, she closed her eyes. "Only a day to get ready, and I have a lesson on John the Baptist."

Claudia was not enthusiastic about teaching a lesson on John, who had never appealed to her. The truth was that she hadn't thought much about him or his role. "John is a victim of benign neglect, as far as I'm concerned," she admitted to herself.

The lesson was a general presentation on John as "the precursor" of Jesus, an ascetic prophet calling his listeners to repent and "make ready the way of the Lord." Claudia was not happy with the basic lesson as it was. It didn't seem suited to the sixth graders she would spend almost an hour with the next day. She felt she had to shape and sharpen the lesson to stimulate the boys and girls, excite their interest, and challenge them.

"John the Baptist," Claudia mused as she stared past the curtains to the streetlight outside. "He's been in the Sunday Gospels the last two weeks." It was Advent. She reached for her Bible as she recalled Father Pritchard's Sunday homily. "He made John real and vibrant," she thought, "and much too challenging."

When Claudia opened her Bible, the question "What then should we do?" jumped at her from the page. "That's the question Father Pritchard kept repeating." With a deeper sense of awareness and purpose, she read the passage. She soon knew how she would present her lesson: it would be around that question.

John the Baptist was called by God to his ministry: to preach repentance and the forgiveness of sins. He would be the "voice" calling people to "prepare a way for the Lord."

But the people were also called by God, and they crowded around John to hear what he was compelled to say: Fear the Lord. Do penance. Be baptized for the forgiveness of sins. Having heard John's preaching and being deeply moved, they might have returned to their families, occupations, and daily concerns resolved to love God and reform their sinful ways. But only for a day or so! The fire of John's message would have glowed briefly and dimmed into extinction. "Not good enough," the people thought to themselves about this preaching. "Too general."

Some of them got up the nerve to pin John down and ask, "What then should we do?" implying that they needed more definite direction. John's response was appallingly simple: "If you have clothing or food that you can share with someone, you should do so."

Tax collectors too put the question to him. "What then should we do?" John could only reply that they be fair and unbiased with all the people they dealt with.

To others who asked the same question came John's third reply: "Treat others kindly. Speak truthfully about others. Put in a fair day's work."

Claudia stared at the Bible page. "Here's some very early preaching that took place during Jesus' lifetime, and the heart of the message is that we treat others with love and justice." She recalled, too, that the prophets hit hard at this theme. Her mouth widened into a smile as she relished the thought of her "discovery." She was pleased, indeed.

She was pleased with this re-awakening, the emphasis that justice and practical love were receiving in homilies, in catechetical books, in diocesan offices, in the bishops' pastoral letters. She was aware too of the critical importance Jesus had placed on these fundamental qualities for living, but now she was taking this what-ought-we-to-do aspect of Christian living back a step further—to John's preaching.

Eager to get her thoughts on paper, Claudia reached for her pad and began to draw up an outline for the lesson. She felt comfortable with her lesson plan as it took shape, because some of what she would teach came from her, was a part of her, and was not entirely from the teacher's manual. She set her mind to presenting her "discovery" to the class in a moving, concrete way: the basic preaching of Christianity demanded that justice and love be part of our everyday lives. "We have only imitation Christianity without it," she said to herself as she turned out the light and walked into the kitchen.

For Reflection and Discussion

1. Does the subject of justice find its way into your classes, even if it is not explicit in your text?

2. Do you teach in generalities and abstractions? Or are you graphic and concrete? Do you give examples to make your teaching memorable and meaningful?

3. Do you prepare your lessons well, given the circumstances you find yourself in?

4. Do you reflect on the lessons you are going to teach, trying to make them more meaningful to you and thereby to your students?

5. Do you tailor each lesson to fit your students' abilities, interests, and concerns?

Prayer

God, as a catechist I'm afraid to ask you, "What should I do?" I know how demanding you can be. But deep down I know what you have called me to do. I ask only, by your grace, that I may be the right tool in your hands to bring the children I teach closer to you. Amen.

19

Mal DeWinter

Is not the bread we break a sharing in the body of Christ? Because the loaf of bread is one, we, though many, are one body, for we all partake of the one loaf.
—*1 Corinthians 10:16–17*

MAL DEWINTER slouched in the folding chair, his legs stretched out and his arms resting on the chairs next to him. He looked over the empty rows of school hall chairs in front of him to the podium where he had just spoken to the parents of second graders. He had planned the three-session program of parent education and arranged for speakers and refreshments. This evening he had welcomed the parents and described the program details.

Now he could sit and drink in the quiet and the satisfaction of what he considered a decent start to this, his fourth year of Eucharist preparation sessions. He had chatted with some parents after his closing remarks and found them pleased, or at least willing to say they'd return to the next session in two weeks. He did sense, however, from the question-and-answer period, some doubt among parents regarding their competence to instruct their children about the Eucharist, and some confusion about "church teachings," a phrase that came up five or six times in their questions.

As Mal walked up to the podium to pick up his papers and head home, Melissa Weigand, a second-grade catechist and one of the Eucharist team, approached him. "How do you feel about tonight, Mal? I'd like to get your reaction."

Mal looked up as he shuffled his papers into his brief case. "I think it went well, and the attendance was pretty good." He walked over to Melissa, who was buttoning up her coat. "You know," he said, "your talk next time will have a lot of interested listeners. It was obvious tonight that there's a need for a theological update. These parents are willing to be part of this, but they're uneasy about the Eucharist. Some of them are comfortable with 'sacrifice,' 'real presence,' 'body of Christ,' and 'Holy Communion,' but not much more. They have motivation; what they need is assurance."

Mal thought highly of Melissa. She did so much studying on her own, but she knew how to temper her enthusiasm and suit her teaching to the present condition of her listeners. She could stretch people's awareness and guide them to expand their vision and test new viewpoints. That's why he wanted her to address the parents at the next session.

"My thoughts are falling into place, Mal. After hearing the questions tonight, I think they'll find a more personal approach to the Eucharist really exciting, and at the same time comforting."

Mal set his brief case and coat on a chair as Melissa went on. "I want to present a broader view of the Eucharist so parents can see First Communion—and help their kids see it—as much more than the isolated act of receiving the consecrated bread and wine. There's more to "communing" at Mass than receiving communion. Communion has its own importance and significance, but over the years we've emphasized it so much we've just about lost sight of other ways of sharing at the Eucharist."

"When it comes to this sacrament, we ask people to believe, but we don't ask them to believe enough," Mal said.

"And in the other sacraments, too," Melissa continued. "In the Eucharist, though, we tend to miss the most visible symbol: ourselves. We gather as the Lord's disciples, sharing a common faith and a common memory of what the Lord has done. We feed one another with our manifestation of faith."

"And as the Gospel reminded us last Sunday," Mal broke in, "we also manifest our spirit of reconciliation, not only with God but with one another. 'Repent and believe,' the Baptist demanded. That sums up the attitude we should bring to the Eucharist. Faith and conversion take place, and then sharing."

Mal glanced over to the refreshment table for any leftovers, but it had already been cleared off. "One less chore to do tonight," he sighed with relief. "People did some sharing over there." He laughed as he pointed to the empty table.

Melissa laughed too. "And think of the sharing we do with God's word. We have the readings that offer us ongoing communication with God and the homily to help us relate God's word to our lives."

After a brief pause, Melissa added, "Then there's the

Creed to express our shared faith, the Prayers of the Faithful to share our individual concerns as well as our common needs. And what could be a more meaningful sharing than the Eucharistic Prayer to praise and thank God for what Jesus has done?"

Mal felt the length of the day begin to work into his body, and he bent over to pick up his coat. "I think you're all set for the next session. You'll be giving the parents the big picture; that's for sure, Melissa. Eucharist preparation is more than First Communion instruction."

"I know," Melissa said as they left the hall and went up the stairs to the outside door. On the landing, Melissa turned to Mal. "But I won't be ignoring First Communion either. In a way, its meaning increases when it's considered in this broader context, as one kind of sharing, however important, among others. It becomes a richer, more intense sharing. I want parents to think of it as the climactic sharing at the Eucharist, when Christians who 'believe and repent' as one body are united with the same Lord."

Melissa stopped as she buttoned up her coat and put her hand on the doorknob. "Ask yourself, 'How much more meaningful would receiving communion become if we grew in our awareness of the other forms of sharing at the Eucharist?'"

She pushed the heavy door open against the January wind and said over her shoulder, "Good night, Mal." He followed, turning to check the door lock. "Good night, Melissa. Let's think some more about your question." As they headed toward their cars, they each left a set of footprints in the new snow.

For Reflection and Discussion

1. In your opinion, what aspect of the Eucharist should be emphasized in a First Communion class?
2. Do you agree with the statement: "Parents have motivation; what they need is assurance"? Why? Why not?
3. As a catechist, are you sensitive to what parents believe—or don't believe—about the sacraments?
4. During your parish liturgies, what "communing" takes place aside from receiving communion?
5. What do you think of Mal's statement: "When it comes to this sacrament, we ask people to believe, but we don't ask them to believe enough"?
6. What sharing might children do in your class to prepare them for the sharing done at the Eucharist?

Prayer

God, you share yourself so intimately with me. Help me to see how I might share myself more with those I teach. Help us all to learn that the sharing we do at the Eucharist will lead to a greater giving of ourselves to you and to all we serve in your name. Amen.

20

J̇EREMY NOVA

> *After Jesus had been born at Bethlehem in Judaea during the reign of King Herod, suddenly some wise men came to Jerusalem from the east asking, "Where is the infant king of the Jews? We saw his star as it rose and have come to do him homage."* —Matthew 2:1–12

JEREMY NOVA felt pretty good about his class, all in all. Absorbed in his thoughts as he left the parish center, he paused at the door, forgetting for a moment where he had parked his car. He had gotten into the habit of reviewing his eighth-grade classes immediately after each session: What went right? Or wrong? How could he improve? And so on. "Not bad," he thought of the day's class as he recalled the students' interest in the Magi.

This early January class had been enjoyable and well received. The feast of the Epiphany was near and the kids were still interested in Christmas stories. They were especially taken with this one—its warm appeal, its charm, its drama. Of course, some of them missed the forest for the trees: "Does Magi mean magicians?" "What's myrrh?" "Why do we call them kings?" "Where'd we get their names?" But overall Jeremy had been pleased by their attention as he told them the story from the viewpoint of Amahl, a shepherd boy.

"...Amahl was almost stiff with fear of being discovered. He didn't know he would have been welcome to join the others as they honored the child. As it was, he thought he had no place there, at least not with those men who were dressed like kings. Amahl stared at the unforgettable scene, awestruck. The baby, the parents, those three men. In the still night, he heard one of them say softly, 'This child is the king of the Jews. We have followed his star....'"

Later that evening, as he was writing his reflections on the afternoon class, Jeremy thought about the richness of that episode in Matthew. He had learned much about it from his catechist formation program and from some reading he did later on. Not that it was all suitable for his eighth graders. "But there's real value in treating the incidentals," he thought. "They're entertaining for one thing, but they're also instructive and can fill out the main picture."

He had been a catechist for six years, and Jeremy shook his head as he remembered the amusing and chaotic things that sometimes happened when he was telling a story or explaining Scripture. One overriding point had come from his experience: he had stopped trying to complete a story or lesson in a given period of time. He should not let this be an end in itself. He had learned to allow for unexpected questions. They could benefit from them if he allowed time to dwell on them. He learned not to move on so fast, not to put off questions until later, but to recognize "graced moments" when the class was ready to learn. "That kind of judgment doesn't come overnight," Jeremy reminded himself.

The clock was striking nine as Jeremy got up to stand by the back window. He was thinking of the questions the kids had asked that day.

"Where did the Magi come from?"

"Were they kings?"

"Where did their names come from?"

"Was there really a star?"

"I know what gold is, but what are frankincense and myrrh?"

Jeremy walked back to his desk with a grin. These had been good questions, and they had helped him get to the heart of the lesson. In class he had implied that it was not important to know whether the Magi events actually happened. But we can know, he made it clear, the meaning behind the events, what the Gospel writer was trying to say.

At the beginning of the Gospel, Jeremy recalled saying, Matthew tells us some very important things about Jesus, and he does this by using some of the customs and beliefs of the time. He wanted the Jewish readers he had in mind, who knew the Old Testament well, to know that Jesus was born in Bethlehem, where the Messiah was to come from. He also emphasized that Jesus, before whom the "kings" kneel, had come not only for the Jews, but for all others as well. He is king of all people, not just the select few. Jeremy recalled Eddie Damon's timely question in class that had helped to bring this point out.

Matthew's audience would also see a connection between the words the Magi used to describe Jesus, "the king of the Jews," and the sign that Pilate had put on Jesus' cross, which carried the same words. By making this connection,

Matthew showed us that the child honored by the Magi was destined to be crucified and raised from the dead. He would become the eternal king of kings.

More than anything else, Matthew wanted his readers to reflect on the infant with his parents and the three men kneeling silently before the Lord, and to ask how we might best pay our homage and open our hearts to Jesus.

"Not a bad class," Jeremy thought, as he sat back. He reflected for a while on the importance of students' questions and the opportunities they present. As he got up and closed his notebook, he noticed that it was almost full.

For Reflection and Discussion

1. Do you read Scripture commentaries to enrich your own understanding and that of your students? Ask your DRE or parish leaders what commentaries are available for your use.

2. When your lesson plan includes Scripture, do you read the passage a few days ahead of time and meditate on it?

3. Do you reflect on your classes to evaluate them and see how you might improve your catechetical skills—both before and after class?

4. Do you ever evaluate how you handle questions, particularly those you find irrelevant, annoying, or insincere? Do you welcome questions as opportunities to teach, or do you consider them "interruptions" of your teaching?

5. Do you sometimes race ahead in order to finish a class "on time," even though you might pass up a beneficial discussion or exercise?

PRAYER

Inspire me, God, with a deep love for your sacred word. May I learn, by your grace, to cherish it in my heart and to be more open to its meaning in my life and in those whom you have called me to teach. Amen.

Subject Finder

Adapting lessons   60, 89–92
Admitting mistakes   68, 72, 82
Advent   90

Beatitudes   42–45

Called to be catechist   1, 4, 9, 54, 77–78, 85
Catechetical courses   1, 11, 17, 18, 46, 81, 99
Conference with DRE   84–88

Day of recollection   1, 21–24, 81
Discipline   1, 8, 13, 17–20, 49, 82
Discouragement   1, 4, 8, 9, 13, 14, 27, 80, 84–85

Enthusiasm   1, 14, 27, 32, 34, 65, 72, 80, 94
Eucharist preparation   93–97
Evaluation of class   49, 98–101

Faith   23, 28, 29, 54, 63, 67, 82, 83, 85, 86, 87, 95, 96
Fresh approaches   42, 51, 52, 94

Growth as catechist   3, 5, 8, 9, 29, 86
Justice   23, 33, 58–58, 91–92

Knowledge of students   12, 26–30, 32, 49, 65–69

Learning from mistakes   12, 14, 18
Lent   48, 51–54, 56–60
Lesson preparation   8, 18, 27, 49, 52, 54, 75, 76, 82, 89–92

Ministry   4, 9, 47, 53, 75–79, 84, 86, 87, 90
Morality education   41–45
Motivating students   8, 17, 54, 57–58, 67–68, 87, 90
Motivation of catechist   1, 47, 52

Parents' meetings and contacts   8, 46, 49, 81, 93–97
Paying the price   8, 13, 32, 33, 34
Prayer   4, 10, 13, 14, 36–40, 46, 51, 52, 57, 61, 82, 83
Presence of God   1, 24, 43, 44, 57, 61, 86

Questions   28, 99, 100

Recruiting catechists   31–35
Reign of God   22–24, 43, 53, 58–60, 101
Resigning, thinking of   7, 14, 27, 80, 81, 84–88
Results of teaching   33, 63, 81, 83

Saints   43, 44, 45
Satisfaction as catechist   6–7, 9, 33, 34, 63, 83, 85, 93, 98, 99
Self-evaluation   71–74, 85, 86, 87
Setting goals   13–14, 23, 24, 34, 80, 85, 86
Sharing with co-catechists   1, 11–12, 19, 23, 26–29, 36–39, 41–44, 46, 48, 57–59, 66, 70–74, 94–96
Silence   19, 36–40
Stories, importance of   2–4, 52, 82, 98, 99
Substitute catechist   89–92

Ten commandments   42, 43
Textbook evaluation   8, 42, 75
Two great commandments   71

(Un)realistic expectations   80, 85, 86
Using Scripture   22, 34, 66, 82, 89–92, 99

Working harder and smarter   47–48, 63, 81, 86, 87